William Francis Gallaway

On the use of with the participle in classical Greek

William Francis Gallaway

On the use of with the participle in classical Greek

ISBN/EAN: 9783337731014

Printed in Europe, USA, Canada, Australia, Japan

Cover: Foto ©ninafisch / pixelio.de

More available books at **www.hansebooks.com**

[illegible]
Classical Greek

A

Dissertation

presented to the Board of University Studies of the Johns Hopkins University for the Degree of Doctor of Philosophy

by

[illegible] Francis Galloway

Baltimore February [illegible]

Table of Contents

Introduction

1 Subject.

2 Scope.

3 General view of ου and μ

4 General view of the participle

5 Combination of the negatives
with the part. expr.

Μή with the participle the
principal verb being expressed:

1 In imperative sentences

2 In optative sentences

3 With verbs of swearing

4 In final sentences

5 In conditional clauses
with εἰ and finite verb expressed

6 In generic relative sentences

7 With the elliptical expression

Μή with the participle in classical Greek

Introduction

the subject

In classical Greek the spheres of οὐ and μή were clearly differentiated but in later times when the appreciation of the delicate shades of meaning conveyed by these negatives had been lost the classical distinction was to a greater or less extent effaced. For example in Greek of the best period μή is the regular negative employed in the protasis of the conditional sentence, the few passages in which οὐ occurs being readily explained in accordance with the laws of the language

cases on either a single word

[illegible]

[illegible] 1

[illegible] the negative of [illegible]

[illegible] Greek [illegible]

[illegible] that of the [illegible] element,

[illegible] regularly followed [illegible] where a fact

[illegible] and [illegible]

[illegible] of [illegible]

[illegible]

X. 37. [illegible] Heb. [illegible]

[illegible] Cor. IX [illegible], XI. 6, XI. 31

James [illegible]

XI. 8, [illegible] Rom. VIII. 9

Modern Greek goes one step further than this and uses the negative [illegible]

[illegible]

---

x. Cf. [illegible]

[illegible]

[illegible] .×

[illegible] reasons &c, [illegible]

[illegible] with [illegible] with [illegible]

[illegible] of the [illegible]

[illegible] pointed out by [illegible]

[illegible] of the

[illegible] 57. They are as follows:

(1) [illegible] with the [illegible] in oratio obliqua, an extension of the classical usage after verba of [illegible];

(2) [illegible] with the finite verb as a form of oratio obliqua [illegible] to avoid [illegible] which frequently lead late writers [illegible] grammatical [illegible] effect;

(3) [illegible] in relative [illegible]

× cf. Mullach, Grammatik der [illegible] Vulgarsprache [illegible]

[illegible] i' [illegible]

[illegible] the [illegible]

took place [illegible] the [illegible]

of [illegible] to be [illegible] defined [illegible]

Greek making an advance on the usage

of the best classical period [illegible]

[illegible] combine any negative but μή

with the [illegible] ×

[illegible] view [illegible] of this gradual ex-

tension and finally universal appli-

cation of μή with the participle it [illegible]

becomes [illegible] important [illegible]

thorough examination of the classical

usage [illegible] order to ascertain how far

later writers were justified [illegible]

[illegible] a small matter in view of the [illegible]

× [illegible] Greek [illegible]

[illegible] will the [illegible] body of classical

[illegible] from [illegible] to [illegible] writers has

been examined and all the instances

of πρίν with the participle noted

From the material so collected we

hope to be able to show how far and

in what connection the writers of the

Greek period of the Greek language made

use of this construction.

It may be well to cite here a list

of the authors examined and editions

[illegible] to

Homer Ameis Hentze,

Hesiod Flach Teubner, 4th

[illegible] Dirok "

Aeschylus Weil " 1884

Sophocles Dindorf Mekler edition "

[illegible] "

[illegible]menta [illegible] [illegible] [illegible]ack.

Teubner, 18[illegible]4.

Aristophanes Bergk 18[illegible]

Fragmenta Comicorum Kock " [illegible] 8

Herodotus Dietsch Kallenberg " 189[illegible].

Thucydides Boehme " [illegible]

Xenophon [illegible]

Cato - Hermann Wohlrab, [illegible]

Orators [illegible]

All bracketed portions of the text and all laws and documents have been omitted unless cited for purposes of comparison. In the case of Hyperides only the speech Υπὲρ Εὐξενίππου has been examined, as the fragmentary state of the others would invalidate any arguments that might be drawn [illegible] the [illegible] sixth volume of Plato containing the spurious [illegible]

[illegible] these [illegible] also [illegible] respect of [illegible] teachers [illegible] useful [illegible] lessons of Plato and [illegible] lines of reasoning have been included, as a [illegible] object [illegible] show the individual usage of any classical author, as the origin and development of the construction the Greek [illegible]

Before entering upon our subject proper it is necessary to discuss briefly three points:—(1) the use of οὐ and μή in classical Greek, (2) the function of the participle, and (3) the combination of the negative with the participle.

I. General [illegible]

[illegible]

[illegible]

[illegible] [illegible] [illegible] [illegible] [illegible]
[illegible] Sanskrit and and Old Persian prohibitive particle mā[1] and we may
perhaps connect it with [illegible] [illegible]
[illegible] sand. The etymology however
gives us very little except the meaning
of μή. But we can afford to dis-
pense with its aid in seeking to de-
termine the classical distinction between
the two negative particles. For indeed,
in Homer there were no contexts [illegible]
and [illegible] there [illegible] no possibility of
confusion.[2] What then are the distinctions
now generally accepted? In brief as
follows: οὐ is the negative of fact,
μή, in accordance with its derivation,

[1] cf. Prellwitz, Etymologisches Wörterbuch [illegible]

[2] Gildersleeve l.c. p. 18

of the use of οὐ is objective and belongs to the things spoken of, μή subjective and refers to the thought and will of the speaker.[1] The broad outlines were fully recognized and clearly marked by the ancients.[2] Negation with οὐ was called ἄρνησις denial. The Etymologicum Magnum says οὐ ἐπίρρημα ἀρνητικὸν καὶ ἀποφατικόν. On the other hand negation with μή was called ἀπαγόρευσις [illegible].

First then let us speak briefly concerning οὐ. Since it is the negative of the statement we find it combined (1) with the indicative of the independent sentence and [illegible]

---

[1] [illegible]

[2] Ety. Magnum 580 [illegible]

[illegible] is coincident with the [illegible] [illegible] ideal of [illegible] [illegible] and [illegible] [illegible] with the past tenses of the indicative [illegible] the potential of the past. These sentences are thus more subjective, but [illegible] are assertions and not mere conceptions and [illegible] take ἄν [illegible];[x] (3) with the subjunctive in Homer [illegible] [illegible] the picture, (4) in questions [illegible] expect an affirmative answer [illegible] used, (5) in subordinate sentences that represent the indicative, i.e. the indicative or optative after [illegible] in oratio obliqua, relative sentences that express a mere statement, temporal, causal, and consecutive sentences with

---

[x] cf. [illegible] p. [illegible]; [illegible] [illegible] Moods and Tenses, §§ [illegible]

[illegible] and the [illegible]

[illegible] and [illegible]

[illegible] represent [illegible]

[illegible] which would have been used

unless the [illegible] of the principal verb

[illegible] sufficient to cause μή, (b) [illegible]

[illegible] used to negative a single word

[illegible] to change it into its opposite e.g.

οὐκ ἐχθές [illegible]. Here it forms

a semi-compound and [illegible].

[illegible] that [illegible] rule [illegible] remains

[illegible] the [illegible] represents [illegible] form

part of a sentence that demands μή.

e.g. cf. Iliad III. 289 foll.

εἰ [illegible] Πρίαμος Πριάμοιό τε παῖδες

τίνειν οὐκ ἐθέλωσιν

[illegible] XIII. 620. εἰ μὲν οὐ πολλοί γε [illegible] ×

× [illegible]

[illegible]

[illegible] ὄχλε [illegible]

[illegible] For examples [illegible]

We have now to the consideration of [illegible] we have [illegible] equality with a [illegible] value of all [illegible] a positive particle, [illegible] accompanied by a [illegible]

[illegible] in the [illegible] of the [illegible] §229 [illegible]

[illegible]

[illegible]

[illegible] produce [illegible] of [illegible]

[illegible] been [illegible] the result [illegible]

[illegible] the earliest [illegible]

[illegible] Greek literature prohibition

expressed by the aorist subjunctive with

μή. The [illegible] appears

only in the [illegible] person plural

cf. Iliad [illegible] 428

[illegible]

[illegible] ἔργον.

[illegible] prohibit [illegible] of μή

with the subjunctive [illegible] appears [illegible]

[illegible] e.g. [illegible]

ΠΕΧΕ μὴ [illegible]

× cf. [illegible]

[illegible]

[illegible] other [illegible] at

[illegible] alt[illegible] [illegible]

[illegible] and [illegible] ally only

[illegible] prohibitive being

always ext[illegible] by mj with the

[illegible] distinction [illegible] had been

taken already by Sanskrit [illegible] of the classical period combined with with the imperative and optative as well as with the injunctive. Mj with the imperative [illegible] [illegible] analogical extension of mj with the [illegible]

The [illegible] mj combined with the optative in the independent [illegible] construction [illegible] [illegible] [illegible] we remember [illegible] optative [illegible] of meaning [illegible]

[illegible]

[illegible]

[illegible] ×

[illegible]

[illegible]

[illegible]

[illegible] take [illegible]

[illegible] likewise [illegible] of will

[illegible] and [illegible]

the [illegible] operative

force and [illegible]

[illegible]

[illegible] either extended [illegible]

that involve the will [illegible] of

meaning, believing, hoping [illegible]

that finally in the early period

[illegible]

× [illegible]

. . . remark. Then in attachment come
in the infinitive after verbs of say
. . . and think of being in refer
. . . relation of . . . locative . . .

. . . a Column

. . . breaking . . . remark
. . . .
the proper negative of . . . . . .

Only with

weak . . . . . . did it take
. . . step and it only appears with
. . . indication . . .

1.E the protasis . . . real . . .
. . . in Bart . . . , rather . . .
. . . anticipate a negative answer,
with . . . and the future in . . .
with verbs of fear when the . . .
present . . . and . . .
. . . with . . .

[illegible] with
participle. It is with the development and use of this construction
that our present [illegible]

We may sum up the uses of μή in
Classical Greek, all of which go back
to the will of the speaker.

In the independent sentence μή is used
with the subjunctive — prohibitions,
the imperative, the optative and past
tenses of the indicative in wishes,
hesitating statement and dubitative
questions, questions that anticipate
a negative answer and [illegible]

In the dependent sentence it is used
after verbs of fear, where the subordinate clause [illegible] only some element
with [illegible] final clauses, the protasis of conditions [illegible]

[illegible]

conditional [illegible] relation [illegible] temporal [illegible] they are equivalent to conditional or [illegible] sentences, with the infinitive when used with [illegible] or after [illegible] expressions that involve [illegible] and finally, with the [illegible] when it represents or forms part of a sentence [illegible]

[illegible]

The combinations of the negative [illegible] and [illegible] should also be considered. But it is not our intention to enter into a full discussion of the negative. We only propose to [illegible] a general view, a brief outline, in order that [illegible] with the [illegible] may [illegible] [illegible]

we [illegible]

a direct bearing [illegible] subject,x

and reverse our position [illegible]

until we [illegible]

[illegible]

General view of [illegible]

Another preliminary [illegible]

value for a brief [illegible]

general view of the participle [illegible]

its employment as a representative [illegible]

The Greeks were [illegible] of the participle and [illegible] a large [illegible]

---

x For treatment [illegible] 202 fol. and [illegible]

[illegible] 1892 [illegible]

[illegible]

[illegible] rupted story [illegible] two directions

[illegible] the actual number of participles

used and (2) [illegible] great freedom

with which the participle is employed

as a substitute for the [illegible]

[illegible] the [illegible] stylistic effect

produced [illegible]

[illegible] connection with our subject

[illegible]

[illegible]

[illegible]

[illegible] suppose that the stories

forms [illegible]

---

cp. Clasen, Beobachtungen über [illegible] sprachgebrauch [illegible]

[illegible] ×

and [illegible]

[illegible]

[illegible]

[illegible]

[illegible]

[illegible]

[illegible]

[illegible]

[illegible]

[illegible]

[illegible]

[illegible]

welchen die gr[illegible]nische Sprache

[illegible] entwickelt [illegible]

[illegible] und [illegible]

[illegible]

[illegible]

[illegible]

[illegible]

[illegible]

[illegible]

[illegible] that all the [illegible]

[illegible] and [illegible]

[illegible] that the [illegible]

these early forms [illegible] still

[illegible] as in later works but still largely adjectival in its character; and

by nothing [illegible] adjectival nature better [illegible]

[illegible] than by the [illegible]

[illegible] by the absolute [illegible]

[illegible] with the [illegible]

Observing therefore that the [illegible]

development of [illegible] participle [illegible]

first Homeric [illegible]

a brief [illegible]

[illegible] without altogether [illegible]

be [illegible] predicable [illegible]
[illegible] at the [illegible]
[illegible] Under [illegible]
[illegible] participle [illegible]
[illegible]
[illegible] adjective e.g. [illegible]
[illegible] XVIII. 12 or with a verbal
or a substantive, e.g. [illegible]
XVIII [illegible] a predicate with
[illegible]
Under these [illegible] read [illegible] these
Cases [illegible] the participle [illegible]
[illegible]
[illegible]
[illegible] spread [illegible]
without exception [illegible]
clause may be –
So the [illegible]
[illegible]

lat [illegible]

proved [illegible] temporal clause we must exclude ἕως [illegible] with the subjunctive, [illegible] represented, and [illegible] clause [illegible] after [illegible] the participle [illegible] participle [illegible] rare [illegible] found chiefly after [illegible] ception [illegible] 2

Under the head of the supplementary participle we must [illegible] those [illegible] which the participle [illegible] the complete the meaning of [illegible]

---

1. cf Kühner Ausführliche Grammatik, [illegible] participle in Euripides [illegible] these exceptions [illegible]

[illegible] οὐ χαίρω [illegible]

[illegible] of an accusative with the

[illegible] λέγω [illegible]

5. Combination of the negative with the participle

After treating separately of the negative and the participle we are now prepared to see how the two were combined.

Whatever was the original feeling of the participle it came to be regarded, in the classical period at least, as an abridged sentence. This is most manifest, perhaps, from the fact that we occasionally find it used with the finite verb [illegible] with a conditional participle [illegible]

[illegible] ὅταν

[illegible]

[illegible]

in the [illegible]culate [illegible] of [illegible]

[illegible] [illegible] [illegible]

[illegible] in participle take [illegible]

the [illegible] nature of [illegible] causal [illegible]

[illegible] [illegible] [illegible] [illegible] participle

ticiple used as an adjective or [illegible]

the representative of causal clauses

relative sentences could naturally

take on since it is then a mere

statement of fact and [illegible]

[illegible] [illegible] [illegible] [illegible]; but on

the other hand when a participle

is used as a substitute for a con-

ditional or a concessive clause it

takes [illegible] as here [illegible] will [illegible]

[illegible] [illegible] [illegible] [illegible]

take [illegible] into [illegible] [illegible] [illegible] the [illegible] [illegible]ce of the [illegible]principal [illegible] [illegible] [illegible]te[illegible]. [illegible] [illegible] [illegible]. 11)

at the [illegible]usage of [illegible] [illegible] [illegible] sometimes sufficient to produce [illegible] [illegible] [illegible] would be more natural. The opposite is also true, for not infrequently the force of the principal [illegible]rb, especially if it is in the imperative mood, is sufficient to cause [illegible] to be used with the participle, although [illegible] would [illegible] more natural [illegible]. [x] This is contrary to the view held by Aken, Gemp[illegible] and Mod[illegible] [illegible] pp. [illegible] and [illegible]27, who asserts that the principal verb has no influence whatever on the negative [illegible].

---

[x] cf. Kühner, [illegible] [illegible] [illegible] [illegible]

particle [illegible] but that the [illegible]
p[illegible] de[illegible] tion [illegible] the nature of [illegible]
particular [illegible] ×σ [illegible] view, however,
is not accepted by other grammarians)
and our investigation will [illegible]
that the principle stated above [illegible]
correct. Of course, when the participle [illegible] only loosely connected with
the main sentence, or [illegible] remote
from the principal verb, or [illegible]
[illegible] intervene, [illegible] original
[illegible] may [illegible]

Having thus, by our discussion of
these preliminary point, [illegible] the
place that [illegible] with the participle
holds [illegible] the development of

× See page 224 where [illegible] den sat[illegible] welch
sie stehen für [illegible] [illegible] [illegible]

and it remains for me to add a detailed examination of the actual occurrences of this construction in classical Greek following the two broad lines that laid down: (1) where the participle forms part of a sentence that demands μή, and (2) where the participle by nature of its own predication takes

M'n with the participle the fundamental

[illegible]

[illegible]

Following the course of the development of [illegible] [illegible]

[illegible] to what extent the participle used in the imperative relative or the imperative sentence [illegible] the force of the principal verb intend when the [illegible] cannot be resolved into an [illegible] [illegible]

In all there are about one hundred and thirty-eight participles [illegible] that form an [illegible] integral part of an imperative clause [illegible] for the sake of [illegible]

[illegible] that those cases [illegible] the
participle agrees with the subject
[illegible] principal [illegible] and [illegible]
[illegible] be resolved into [illegible]
[illegible]; secondly, where the participle [illegible] the [illegible]
either with or without [illegible]; thirdly,
where the participle is in the predicate either taking the place of an
object clause, or agreeing with the
object of the verb; fourthly where
the imperative appears in an
direct form after verbs like
κελεύω, [illegible] the participle
being connected with the subordinate clause [illegible] really belongs under
the head of the [illegible] but is
being an indirect [illegible]
perative [illegible].

[illegible] other cases [illegible]

cases which [illegible] [illegible]

included [illegible]

It has [illegible]

[illegible] eighty, [illegible]

one hundred and thirty exam[illegible]

It does not appear [illegible] but the

examples are found [illegible]

[illegible] and [illegible] 96, and should [illegible]

The first passage reads

[illegible] γυναῖκα [illegible] ἦγε [illegible]

μηδέ [illegible] μάλα πόλλ' [illegible]

μηδ' [illegible] μάλα πολλά

[illegible] is equivalent to [illegible]

The other passage [illegible]

(Such cases as Hom. Od. iii 96,

μηδέ τί μ' αἰδόμενος μειλίσσεο μηδ' ἐλεαίρων,

have not been included as here the

negatives go with the verb and no

the infinitive. For similar examples, cf. [illegible] of Od. [illegible] 231, Soph. Antig. 264, Eur. Hecuba 973, [illegible] 266 [illegible]

We have also excluded passages like [illegible] Meno [illegible] κεφάρισιν [illegible] [illegible] ἔλεγχον [illegible] λόγον [illegible], [illegible] the position of the negative shows that it belongs to the following substantive ideas and not to [illegible]

Similar examples are: Il. iv. 46, [illegible] iii 255, Plato Crito [illegible] Phaedrus 260 C, Meno [illegible], Rep. IV, 16[illegible] C, VII 534 C, Laws VII [illegible]

Moreover, not only in the case of the imperative but also in regard to other constructions that follow we have omitted those examples in which [illegible]

. ticiple a [illegible] d [illegible]

f..d with [illegible] of [illegible]

[illegible]

[illegible] μὴ [illegible] πρὸς [illegible]

[illegible] παρέχοι (Thuc [illegible])

n lyric poetry especially [illegible] the [illegible]

tary elegies of Tyrtaeus and Theognis

the use of the participle with the imp[illegible]

ative is more common. [illegible]

[illegible] been noted e.g. [illegible]

[illegible] μὴ [illegible]

[illegible]

Of the tragedians Aeschylus and Sophocles

make but slight use of the participle [illegible]

a substitute for the imperative.

[illegible] has but two examples [illegible]

[illegible] both Electra [illegible]

[illegible]

[illegible]

n ia l.ifle ueal l a l

ireading in the ratio (a d hours be. a in

la. following infinitive) the r sate

in py, not ee

(infinitive more freq the use of

the acc. h cotion and have elecu u

stances en it. n some cases the

verb have to be supplied from the

. , as ( ) with

ὡς μόνον ἄνδρα ἐπιεικέστερον

where ἄνδρα to be supplied fro

Note upon Stra

ctidae, 163, where μή is due to the

prohibitive force of the sentence

ΔΗ. οὔκουν ἐγὼ μὲν ἔβλεπον εἶναι κύριος;

ΚΟ. ἔλεγον ὑγιαινούσας μηδέν

Inc omedes we find a few cases of

participle in used . . . or

not lout . . . . story

in the [illegible] Xenophon

historical works [illegible]

Thucydides [illegible]

all but one of which occur in speech

in the other writings of Xenophon [illegible]

examples are found [illegible]

are in the Cynegeticus which [illegible]

[illegible]

[illegible] orators Antiphon, Andocid-

[illegible] Isaeus, [illegible], and Lyc-

urgus do not use it at all, Isocra-

tes has four examples, three of which

are in the first speech which is

generally regarded as spurious, [illegible]

mosthenes, [illegible], and [illegible]

[illegible] This small [illegible]

of passages [illegible] orators [illegible]

the [illegible]

[illegible] [illegible]

[illegible] of [illegible] [illegible] of [illegible] expression would seem [illegible] record with Müller, Chr. [illegible] 1402, but we must remember that the orator was not meant to use the imprecation at all, except under stress of emotion and then the bare imprecation is more appropriate than a participle which belongs rather to a leisurely manner of utterance and not to passionate language.

Catullus largely and [illegible] expect to find a large [illegible] of examples. [illegible] I recall [illegible] fifteen of which occur in the [illegible]. Many dialogues have only [illegible] instance, many [illegible] [illegible] [illegible]

[illegible]

κρουων ὡς λόγος, ἀλλ' οὐκ [illegible] [illegible]

τοῖσι λόγοισι [illegible] [illegible]

the imperative, while ἐπιφέρων and

ἐθέλων are merely disconnected parti-

ciples. Ukens, in accordance with

his theory, would doubtless say that

the difference in the negatives is due

to this fact. But we frequently

find οὐκ ἐθέλω coalescing into a

quasi compound and remaining

unchanged in spite of it [illegible]

[illegible] and that this cannot [illegible] repre-

sentation of which [illegible] might

Again note Gorgias 463 A, εἰπὲ μοι [illegible]

ἐμὲ [illegible], which Ukens, l. c.

quotes as an example of the final

participle. It [illegible]

as we can see [illegible]

[illegible] construction of the [illegible] [illegible]
[illegible] 690 have [illegible] [illegible] and
16. 277 E λέγε μηδὲν [illegible] Even
[illegible]

In [illegible] we have [illegible] with
the participle equivalent to [illegible]
with the finite verb [illegible] γεγνώ-
κοντες [illegible] ὁ [illegible]
[illegible] ἔχοντες [illegible]

For other examples of this construction
cf. Aeschylus Sup. 269. Eurip. Ino. 1166. Matt.
IX. 45, Mc. II. 2. 3. 44 [illegible] XX. 20
Plato, Laws [illegible]

For convenience of reference and also
to show at a glance the range of
construction a complete list of the
passages in which that construction
is found [illegible] appended to each section.

[illegible]

[illegible] the [illegible] [illegible] not [illegible]

[illegible]

[illegible]
[illegible] 196 f
[illegible] 98
[illegible] Tacu[illegible]
X [illegible]
XII [illegible]
XV [illegible]
[illegible]
VII 14
[illegible]
[illegible]
[illegible]
[illegible]
[illegible]
[illegible] 18 [illegible]
[illegible]
[illegible] 510
90[illegible]
Sophocles
[illegible] 10[illegible]
[illegible]

E[illegible]
Alcestis 109[illegible]
[illegible] 874
Heraclidae 175
263
619
[illegible] 105
1110
[illegible] 140
409
818
Medea 1122
Cy[illegible] 657
[illegible] 723
[illegible] 1234
[illegible] 286 [illegible]
779
Comici Minores
Chrecerates 8[illegible]
Strattis 37
Antiph[illegible] 52 [illegible]
[× Menander 178.3
Demonax 2[illegible]]

T[illegible]
I 12 [illegible]
II [illegible]
III 40.7
48.1
IV 17.3
V. 20.[illegible]
VI[illegible] 77.5
Xenophon
Cyr. III. 1 37
VII 5. 20
Cyr II 1
IV. [illegible]
VI. 1[illegible]
[illegible]
X [illegible]
Isocrates
I. 13. 17. 47
III 57
Demosthenes
XXII. 47
Aeschines
III. 247

Demosthenes
III 20
Plato
Theaet 153 E
Sophist 239 B
240 a
247 B
Politicus 263 E
269 C
277 E
Philebus 14 B
28 D
58 D
Laches 189 B
Protag 33[illegible]
Gorgias 463 A
Hip. Mai 298 D
[illegible]
Laws. VI. 754 A
VII. 818 E
VIII. 828 B
84[illegible]

849 E
IX. 868 C
871 a
879 D
882 B
X 887 C
XI 919 D
922 C
XII 943 C
95[illegible]

Our second division of μή with the participle in [illegible]

× The examples from the New Comedy have been [illegible] for the sake of completeness [illegible] have not [illegible] however [illegible]

is that in which the participle [illegible] the genitive absolute [illegible] class is much smaller than the preceding and does not [illegible] μή οὐ in fact being found almost as frequently as [illegible]

This is doubtless due, in most cases, to the fact that the genitive absolute is not felt to be as closely connected with the principal verb as when the participle agrees with the subject. In others we can see a special reason for the retention of οὐ

The genitive absolute in this construction is generally preceded by ὡς, but one exception to this rule being [illegible] Hdt. VII. 10δ. οὐ ἐῶν μὴ βούλευ ἐς κίνδυνον μηδένα τοιοῦτον ἀπικέσθαι, μηδεμιῆς ἀνάγκης ἐούσης, ἀλλὰ [illegible] Here the participle is temporal or causal [illegible]

... must be due to the force of the imperative.

For an example with ὡς cf. Aristoph. Frogs 28. ΗΡΑ βούλει καί τι κακὸν ... φρόνει;

ΔΙΟ. ... ὡς ἄν ... γε μὴ βαδίζω ...

Here we must supply φράζε from the preceding line. Μὴ, it is true, goes with βαδίζω ..., but still it is a good example of the influence of the imperative. For other examples cf. Thuc. VII. 15. Hdt. 44. 7. Xen. Cyr. I. 6. 11. Plato, Phaedo, 7... Phaedr. 176 B. Rep. I. 327 C. Laws. XI 915 E. (Menander ...

... example ... Laws, 77 E. ... rather ... ὡς ... (ἡμῶν) ... μᾶλλον ... ὡς ἡμ... ... the whole phrase ὡς ἡμ... ... contrasted with the preceding ...

[illegible] the [illegible]

this construction is conversational, the example from Isaeus being the only exception, hence we are not surprised to find that it does not occur in the orators.

In the four examples that follow ὡς οὐ with the participle in the genitive absolute is connected with an imperative. In three of the cases the imperative follows and its force is felt less than if it prec[illegible]. It must be noticed also that ὡς with the participle is virtually a form of oratio obliqua and as such its natural negative is οὐ not μή;[x] this may help to account for [illegible]

---

[x] cf Gildersleeve [illegible]

[illegible] of [illegible] [illegible]
as follows: Eurip. Medea 3[illegible]

ὡς οὐκέτ᾽ ὄντων τῶν τέκνων φρόντιζε δή.

Here also the negative of fact may be retained as commonly when speaking [illegible] Xen. Mem. II 6. 32.

ὡς οὐ προσοίσοντος τὰς χεῖρας δίδασκε

here a whole line intervenes between the participle and the finite verb.

ib. Cyr. VIII. 4. 27, ὡς ἀναμενοῦντος καὶ οὐκ ὑποδεχομένου οὕτω παρασκευάζου.

Plato Apol. 30 B. ἢ ἀφίετε ἢ μὴ ἀφίετε ὡς ἐμοῦ οὐκ ἂν ποιήσοντος ἄλλα

The force of the assertion in the last case is evident.

In the third class of μή with the participle in imperative sentences are included those cases in which the participle appear as the object of

[illegible] [illegible] [illegible] [illegible] [illegible]

[illegible] a [illegible] to [illegible] the participle frequently takes the place of an object clause and hence, owing to the peculiarity of the Greek idiom may be in the nominative, when its subject is the [illegible] as that of the [illegible] [illegible]. When not used as an object clause it agrees with the object of the [illegible]. ὡς is sometimes used with the participle but more frequently

The first example noted [illegible] in Aeschylus, [illegible] [illegible]

ἄλευ, πόνων εἴκηνε μὴ [illegible] [illegible]

where μὴ [illegible] is equivalent X to [illegible] [illegible]

Another example in Agam. 9[illegible]

[illegible] μὴ [illegible] [illegible]

erse ...

...

it is hard to decide whether we have the participle or the infinitive, as both are the same form. Baumlein ... r. p. 268, takes it as the participle. Sophocles has five examples of the construction, four of which have ... The passages are: Antig. 1063, 1064, O.C. 1155, Phil. 1013, 1015. In the last example μή is used in spite of the fact that it refers to one ...

... ἀναρπάσει ...

cf. Hdt. III. 65, where the same construction occurs and where ... grammatically, it seems to me, object ...

Euripides has but ...

[illegible] th Co in [illegible] [illegible] leingth cited, [illegible] the most noteworthy [illegible] particular, 693.

[illegible] μή [illegible] ἔφυνε [illegible]

[illegible] οὐχ [illegible]

[illegible] ἀλλὰ [illegible]

[illegible] Reiske quoted by Elmsley, make the participle depend on ἔφυνε, others supply ἴσθι, but Elmsley himself and most other editors take the participle as the consecutive absolute. We still however, have to account for the [illegible] and a sufficient explanation may doubtless be found in the imperative force of the sentence without supplying a definite verb. See [illegible]

[illegible] ὡς πρὸς [illegible]

[illegible] καὶ μὴ [illegible] [illegible]

[illegible]

[illegible]

[illegible] blouged [illegible] exactly th[illegible]

[illegible Greek]

It seemed therefore that in the case of the accusative absolute as in that of the genitive absolute, the same choice of negatives is permitted

[illegible] belongs under this head we have to supply the imperative from the preceding [illegible]

K.P. [illegible Greek]

ΙΩΝ. [illegible Greek]

"[illegible] pity me who know neither mother nor father"

[illegible]

[illegible]

Aeschylus	Euripides	Comici Minores	Xenophon	Aeschines
Sup. 209	Andromache 726	Antiphanes 177	Cyr. IX. 15	I 161
Agam. 937	Heraclidae 693	Philemon Fr.	Isocrates	Plato
Persae 1131	987	[illegible]	V. 133	Gorgias
Sophocles	Ion 313	Herodotus	Demosthenes	
OC 1155	Tragici Minores	III. 65	XXVII 57	
Antig 1063. 1064	Frag. incert. 122	VIII 144	[illegible]	
Phil. 253 n 15	quoted by Dem.	Thucydides		
	XVIII 287	I 141		

Μή is not invariably found in this construction. Indeed as the participle here is a form of oratio obliqua we should rather expect to find [illegible]. [illegible] it seems to point to the strong influence of the imperative that in so many of the cases have μή and [illegible] (See [illegible]) The example with οὐ has already been cited from Eurip. [illegible] Soph. Phil 567.

[illegible]

That this is [illegible]

[illegible] three [illegible]
tween the principal verb and the [illegible]
[illegible] and hence [illegible] not changed
Cb. 2.122.2, ὥστε οὐκ ἄλλοις φέρουσιν [illegible]
[illegible] δουλείαν Demos. XXII 39 [illegible]
οὐ [illegible]

We see then from these few passages
that although [illegible] is permitted with the
participle in the construction the
tendency is to assimilate the negative
to that of the imperative.

Our fourth class of μή with the participle in imperative sentences includes
what we have called the indirect
imperative, namely, where the participle forms part of an [illegible]
clause depending on verbs of exhortation, or command [illegible]

... not ... example ... Euripides

Frag. 311, καὶ νῦν παρῄνεσα πᾶσι τοῖς νεωτέροις

μὴ πρὸς ἰσχύος ἀποβολὰς κειμένοις,

σχολῇ ... [illegible]

Aristoph. Clouds, 966. the next example ... characteristic ... εἶτ' αὖ προμαθεῖν ᾆσμ' ...

... τὼ μηρὼ μὴ ξυνέχοντας

Other examples are Hdt. I. 80, 170, Thuc. I. 82. 1, 140. 3; IV. 35. 3, 98. 8; VIII 14. 1, Xen. Anab. IV 3. 25, Dem. XV. 4, (LIX. 75.) νόμον ... αὐτὴν εἶναι καὶ μὴ ἐπιμεμιγμένην ἑτέρᾳ ...

Plato, Laws, III 702 C. VII. 810 E, XI. 9 ...

We see, therefore, from these examples that the construction ... In one or two cases οὐ seems to be used contrary to the ...

... cf. Hdt. IX. 122: ... ... κελεύων παρασκευάζεσθαι ὡς οὐκέτι ἄρξοντας ἀλλ' ἀρξομένους

[illegible] ὑπέρ με Καπανέως [illegible]
[illegible] χρήματα φρίσσοντας [illegible] καὶ ἀνήκοπας [illegible]
γειν ὡς [illegible] μεθ' [illegible]

It is to be noticed that in both of these passages the participle is preceded by ὡς, while in all the examples cited above we have the simple participle. This may account for the retention of οὐ. In the latter case also we have the accusative absolute, which, as we have already [illegible] permits οὐ after an imperative.

A few passages still remain to be discussed [illegible] which μή is apparently due to the force of the imperative, but which cannot well be classed under any of the above heads. [illegible]

ἀλλ' ὅδε μέντοι [illegible] [illegible]
γίγνου [illegible] [illegible]

[illegible] . κάμ[illegible] μ[illegible] μὴ ἔχοντας [illegible] [illegible] explained as dep[illegible] [illegible] the preceding imperative [illegible] [illegible] [illegible] in English [illegible] The participle [illegible] owever, seems rather to express result and [illegible] may be right in saying that it depends on some subordinate idea, as ὥστε μὴ μεθέξειν [illegible] [illegible] Cyn VI.5, [illegible] δὲ [illegible] ὁ ἀρκυωρὸς ἐξίτω ἔχων ἀπὸ [illegible] μὴ ἔχοντα [illegible], The force of the imperative is here evident, and also in Antiphon, [illegible] δ 10, μήτε [illegible] [illegible] μὴ προσηκούσας συμφορὰς ἐμβάλητε. cf also Plato. Laws. VIII. 833[illegible] 841 [illegible]

This then finishes our treatment of μή with the participle in the imperative sentence. We see that the force of the principal verb is [illegible] [illegible] [illegible]

ficit to produce ui in the subordi-
-nate clause, even like the participle
cannot be resolved into an imp
and would, under other circumstances
be required to [illegible]. A few exceptions
to this rule have been noted but their
number is small in comparison
with those that take ui, and many
[illegible] admit of a satisfactory explanation on other grounds.
Putting the results of the foregoing
pages into a tabular form we
get the following table.

N. with the subject and importance

Authors	He agreeing with subject	He ... Clue	He agreeing with object	... not importance
Homer				
Hesiod				
Lyric poets other than Pindar	1			
Pindar	1			
Aeschylus	2		3	
Sophocles	3		5	
Euripides	16		4	1
Tragici Minores			1	
Aristophanes		1		1
Comici Minores	3*(2)		17*(2)	
Herodotus	-	1	2	2
Thucydides	7	3	1	1
Xenophon	7	1	1	1
Orators	7		4	3
Plato	30	4	1	3
Total	85(2)	10	33*(2)	[illegible]

* From the New Comedy

2 In Optat.

From the imperative we come next to μή with the participle in wishes, including both the optative and the past tenses of the indicative.

The dividing line between the optative and the imperative is often very faint. As the imperative may express a command, an exhortation, and an entreaty so the optative may express various shades of feeling from that which comes very close to a command to the most humble prayer (e.g.)

The negative of this independent optative is μή. Hence a participle that represents such an optative or forms an integral part of a clause depending on it must also be negatived by μή. Examples of participles so used are:

it … … … … and they are found in all periods of the language from Homer on. Then fall most readily into two classes; first the direct wish, where the principal verb is in the optative or indicative, and the participle either agrees with the subject, or the object or some subordinate word; and secondly the indirect wish, where the sentence forms part of an infinitive clause after verbs of praying or wishing, … … We take them …

The single passage in Homer … construction is found …

μὴ μνηστεύσαντες μηδ' ἄλλοσ' ὁμιλήσαντες ὕστατα καὶ πύματα νῦν ἐνθάδε δειπνήσειαν "May they (after their wooing …

[illegible] to [illegible] [illegible]
[illegible]

[illegible] another passage [illegible] what similar to this in Od. xi. 613.

μὴ τεχνησάμενος μηδ' ἄλλο τι τεχνήσαιτο

Here however, μὴ does not go with τεχνησάμενος but merely, as a sort of free negative, serves to introduce the whole sentence.

Hesiod has three examples of this construction Works and Days 444, 458 sq. 444 ff.

τοῖς δ' ἅμα τεσσαρακονταετὴς αἰζηὸς ἕποιτο
ὅς κ' ἔργου μελετῶν ἰθεῖαν αὔλακ' ἐλαύνοι,
μηκέτι παπταίνων μεθ' ὁμήλικας

The generic sentence that introduces [illegible]

For full discussion of the passage see [illegible] Hentze, [illegible], and Cauer.

[illegible] ti
ance of the negative.
Theognis is the only one of the lyric poets who uses the participle with μή in this construction. He has two examples: v. 1150 & 1176. The first reads:
εἴη μοι πλουτεῦντι κακῶν ἀπάτερθε μεριμνῶν
ζώειν ἀβλαβέως μηδὲν ἔχοντι κακόν.
The other example is similar.
Neither Aeschylus nor Sophocles has any instances of the participle with μή, but Euripides has several instances. Note Alcestis, 536, which shows still another position of the participle:
εἰ ηὔχομαι σ' [illegible] μὴ λυπούμενον.
Aristophanes has one example, Lysias one, Demosthenes two, if we include XXIV. 171. οἱ δ' [illegible] ἂν εἰκότως μὴ εἴη πάντες ἄκοντες οἱ δ' ἀναίτιοι καὶ [illegible]

xiv. [illegible] Aroferia[illegible] [illegible],

when μή [illegible] to be due to the general optative tone running through the whole [illegible]. Or, if this explanation is not satisfactory, we may adopt that employed in somewhat similar cases by Stuker in [illegible] and take μή with the following infinitive. The complete list of passages in which this construction occurs was [illegible]

Homer	Theognis	Critias 1580	Comici Minores	Lysias
Od. IV. 684	1152	Frag. 201	Eubulus 72.5	XXIV. 26
	1156	360. 27	Incert. 151.	Demosthenes
Hesiod	Euripides	399	(Diphilus. 73.9	XX. 109
Op. et D. [illegible]	Alcestis 536	Aristophanes	Eurip. [illegible]	XXIV. 171
489	Sph. 518	Plutus, 592	535)	(Plato
5[illegible]	Ion. 5[illegible]			Laws VII 823E

The wish, as is well known, is characteristic of Euripides and we have a confirmation of it here in the frequent use as compared with other writers, of μή with the participle in optative [illegible]

Notice also the utter absence of the construction from the historians and its
small use in prose generally. The
writers, however, have but little oppor-
tunity for using this optative so that
their small use of the participle is not
surprising [illegible]

In Euripides, Helena, 730, ου seems to be
employed contrary to the general rule:

ἐγὼ μὲν εἴην, κεἰ πέφυχ᾽ ὅμως λάτρις,
ἐν τοῖς γενναίοισιν ἠριθμημένος
δούλοισι, τοὔνομ᾽ οὐκ ἔχων ἐλεύθερον

The participial clause is not felt as an
integral part of the wish, hence the
negative of [illegible] [illegible]

Under the second head of μή with
the participle in optative sentences are
included those passages in which
the participle forms part of [illegible]

t[illegible] [illegible] certa[illegible] of b[illegible]

(Sq[illegible], as in the case of the indirect imperative, we have, strictly speaking, a subdivision of the infinitive construction, but the general optative tone of the sentence warrants us in classifying them under this head.

The first instance of this construction is in Pindar, Pythia. IV 292 εὔχεται οἶκον ἰδεῖν μή ποτε [illegible] τινι πῆμα πορών, [illegible] ὁ αὐτὸς πρὸς [illegible].

The next is Soph. O.O. 1509.

θέλω πόλιν σε τήνδε μὴ φεύγειν [illegible]

Other examples are: Eurip. Iph Au. 378 (βούλομαι), Aristoph. Knights, 766 (εὔχομαι), Lysis. 474 (θέλω), Thuc. II 2.3, ἐβούλοντο in Πλάταιαν ἔτι τ' ἐν εἰρήνῃ τε καὶ τοῦ πολέμου μήπω φανεροῦ καθεστῶτος προκαταλαβεῖν.

The participial clause is part [illegible]

... and ... ... about ... with ... ... ib. VIII. 92. 11. (οὐκ ᾔδεσαν), Xen. Cyr. 1. 4. 26 (βούλομαι), Hell. VI. 2. 39 (βούλομαι) Lysias VIII. 2 (βουλόμενον ἂν), Isoc. VI. 8 (ἐδεόμην ἂν), Xen. XV. 12 (βούλομαι) ... ... Plato, ... 195 ... ...

In tabular form ... the use of μή with the participle ... wishes is as fol...

Authors	Direct	Indirect	Authors	Direct	Indirect
Homer	1		Aristophanes	1	2
Hesiod	3		Comici Minores	1	
Lyric Poets, not including Pindar	2		Herodotus		
Pindar		1	Thucydides	—	
Aeschylus			Xenophon		2
Sophocles		1	Orators	3	2
Euripides	8	1	Plato	1	1
Totals	14	3	Totals	6	

3. With verbs of swearing.

Closely allied with the use of μή in the expression of a wish is its use with verbs of swearing, in which the will of the speaker is also exerted. In a very few passages, only four or five in all, we find a participle with μή forming part of an infinitive clause after such verbs. This construction is again but a [illegible] of the use of the participle with the infinitive, which will be [illegible], but its connection with the indirect optative just discussed is sufficient excuse for placing [illegible]

[illegible] Nemea VII. 71, furnishes the first example. [illegible]

μή τέρμα προβὰς ἄκονθ' ὥτε χαλκοπάραον ὄρσαι

this a
reading the ... which
Christ adopts and which would ...
μή to be taken with ... Bergk and
Bury, however, accept the reading given
which seems on the whole to be
preferable.
The other passages in which the
construction occurs are Eurip. Iph.
..., Aristoph. ..., Antipho
..., Xen. Cyr. VI. 1. 3. μή goes with
both participle ... ἀπειρηκότων
ἢ μὴν μὴ ὑπὸ τοῦ ... παιδὸς
... γιγνώσκειν,
In Antiphon I 28, there is some doubt
as to the correct reading ... σο
... ὑπὲρ τῆς μητρὸς ...
πεποιηκυῖαν ταῦτα. This is the reading of Blass, who follows ...

... ...

The rarety of the participle in this construction is doubtless due to the fact that verbs of swearing are not very frequently employed by the classical writers, ... opportunities for using it are infrequent.

2. In ... Sentences

Having thus far treated the participle with μή as the representative of the imperative, the wish, and the oath, all of which are capable of being expressed as independent sentences, we turn now to its use in de... ... Here ...

... ... μή ... the ... tive used ... ...

...ality ... con... ... ...

... ... participle ... ...

longs to ... of sentence, must a... be negatived by μή.

Let us first take up the final ... tence, including besides the ... final, object clauses after verbs of ... ving for, or effecting, and after ... The number of participles ... used is not very large, and they do not appear before the time of Aeschylus. In the majority of cases the final ... ticle is expressed, but in some instances μή seems to be due to the general idea of purpose running through ...

The first example noted ... Aeschylus ... ...

ὅπως [illegible] μὴ [illegible] κλύον μου

S. Soph. Ajax 472 the final [illegible] is not expressed, but μή depends on the general idea of purpose

πεῖρά τις ζητητέα

τοιάδ᾽ ἀφ᾽ ἧς γέροντι δηλώσω πατρὶ

μή τοι φύσιν γ᾽ ἄσπλαγχνος ἐκ κείνου γεγώς.

Examples of object clauses are:- Xen. Cyr. VIII.1.42, ἐμελέτησαν ὡς μὴ ἱδρῶντες μηδὲ ἀπομυττόμενοι φανεροὶ εἶεν, μηδὲ μεταστρεφόμενοι ἐπὶ θέαν μηδενὸς ὡς οὐδὲν θαυμάζοντες. The last clause with οὐ is rather peculiar, following, as it does, so many clauses with μή but the construction changes here and it is not felt as an integral part of the sentence, so that οὐ is reg.

ib. Rep. Lac. VI.1. Isoc. VI.94, XX. [illegible]

περὶ τοῦ εἶναι Νικίᾳ ὅπως [illegible]

ἀλλότρια ἴσχυρ[illegible]ο, ἀλλ' ὅπως μὴ μηδὲν ἀδικῶν κακὸν [illegible] πείσεται. This is the reading of Bekker, and Müller and [illegible] Blass read ὅπως μὴ οὐδὲν κτέ. The Mss. have simply ὅπως μηδὲν ἀδικῶν. The sense seems to require the participle [illegible] [illegible] [illegible] and it is easier to see how μή could have been dropped with μηδέν than [illegible] [illegible]. So that [illegible] prefer to read ὅπως μὴ μηδὲν [illegible]. Other examples of object clauses are: Xen. V. 13, VIII. 13, (X 41). Plato, Laws, [illegible]

Of μή with the participle depending on a verb of fear but one example [illegible] [illegible] [illegible], namely Plato Char. 166 D φοβούμενος μή ποτε λάθω οἰόμενος μέν τι εἰδέναι, εἰδὼς δὲ μή. ου properly follows μή after verbs of fear. Cf. Thuc. VII. 20. 7 [illegible] μὴ οὐ προιδόντες [illegible] [illegible]

[illegible] περιφάλη[illegible] [illegible], where it belongs to the participle, but may sometimes be found[×] and this seems to be an instance of the [illegible] [illegible] Theages 122 C; the participle forms part of a cautious assertion, the verb of fear not being expressed. cf. Antiphon V 75.

The list of passages in which the participle forms part of a final clause is as follows:

Aeschylus	Thucydides	XVII. 47	XIX. 35	Euthyd. 30[illegible]
Pro. 824	IV. 67. 4	XXI. 13	XX. 136	Laws
Sophocles	Xenophon		XXIV 28	
Ajax 472	Anab. VII. 2. 33	Isaeus	(LXI. 10)	
O.R. 1389	Cyr. IV 6. 11	V 5		
O.C. 1279	VIII. 1. 42	VIII 4	Plato	
Herodotus	Rep. Lac. VI 1	Demosthenes	Alcib. I. 122a	
IV 139	Cyn. X. 1	V. 13	(Theages 122c)	
[illegible]	Isocrates	VIII 13	Char. 166d	
	V 71	(X. 41)		
		(XVII. ?)		

(As in the preceding classes, so in the

× cf. Goodwin Moods and Te[illegible]

occasionally found where we should expect μή, but it can generally be explained on the principle of adhaerescence. So Soph. Electra 584,

εἰ δ' ὁρᾷ μὴ σκῆψιν οὐκ οὖσαν [illegible]

[illegible] Eurip. Troc. 1319 [illegible]

[illegible] οὐκέτ' ὄντα [illegible]

Hdt. I. 99. ὅκως ἂν μὴ ὁρῶντες οἱ ὁμήλικες, ἐόντες οἰκίης οὐ φλαυροτέρης οὐδὲ ἐς ἀνδραγαθίην λειπόμενοι, λυπεοίατο.

οὐ φλαυροτέρης can be explained on the principle of adhaerescence, then ὄντες follows as a matter of [illegible]

Thuc. VIII. 45. 2 ἵνα αὐτῶν μὴ οἱ ναῦται ἐς ναῦς ἀπολείπωσιν οὐχ ὑπολιπόντες τὸν μισθόν. The Mss. vary in regard to οὐχ, some omitting it, others retaining it and still others having μή on the margin. The majority of editors retain οὐχ.

may be explained on the ground of the causal nature of the participle and its distance from μή [illegible]

Dem. XXIX, 46 (cited by Aiken, p. 229) seems to be a real exception — ἵν᾿ ἐξ εἰκότος ὧν οὐδὲν προσῆκον ἡμῖν ἔχειν. The other passage cited by Aiken is Dem. Proem. [illegible] is easily explained as above. It reads ἵνα — δι᾿ αὐτόν, ἀλλὰ μὴ δι᾿ ὅμως οὐκ ἐθέλοντας ἀκούειν τοῦτο πε- ριδέναι [illegible]

5 — In Conditional Clauses with εἰ and Finite Verb Expressed.

Next after the final sentence we take the use of μή with the participle in the conditional proposition. There are two broad divisions:— first, where the conditional particle and [illegible]

rb are expressed the participle serving to introduce some parallel or subordinate idea; and secondly, where the participle itself forms the protasis of a conditional proposition. The latter is much the larger class and constitutes the main development of μή with the part[illegible].

But at present we are only treating those cases of the participle in which the principal verb is expressed, so that we must now confine ourselves to the [illegible]

About two hundred and seventy nine instances of this construction have been noted. The first example is found in the "[illegible]", but after Homer it does not occur again

[illegible]

[illegible] one that it is found [illegible] frequently and [illegible] all department of the language. As the conditional sentence belong largely to argumentative discourse, so its use of the participle abounds in the Orators, some of the dialogues of Plato, and in writing, like the Memorabilia

[illegible]

The participle appears in a variety of forms sometimes in the nominative, agreeing with the subject of the principal verb, sometimes in the genitive absolute, and again as the object of the [illegible]

Then, true to his theory that the principal verb does not influence the participle, [illegible] often put to great straits to [illegible] [illegible] [illegible] So [illegible] respect to [illegible] [illegible] [illegible] [illegible]

. or μὴ εἶσο... ...sagt "nicht weil μὴ ἐὰν, sondern weil der acc. c. ptc. einem acc. c. inf. gleichsteht; möglich gewählt aber weil der Sinn ist ἐὰν ... μὴ εἰδῇς καὶ ..." and in respect to Dem. XXXI. 5 he says, "εἰ φανείη μὴ λαχὼν ... εἰ μὴ ... λαχὼν." It seems much simpler, however, to explain the μὴ as being due to the influence of the principal verb rather than to resort to such roundabout explanation.

As this class does not present many difficulties, after citing a few examples by way of illustration, we shall simply give the complete list of occurrences ... under each ...

The first example noted ...

... ...

[illegible] ἔκαστος [illegible] ἀκούσῃς μηδ' [illegible]

The next example is Soph. Ajax, 1317.

ἄναξ Ὀδυσσεῦ, καιρὸν ἴσθ' ἐληλυθώς,
εἰ μὴ ξυνάψων, ἀλλὰ συλλύσων πάρει.

The participles here express purpose, and μή might possibly be due to this cause, but the other explanation is simpler.

Notice again Trach. 411.

ΑΓ. [illegible] ποίαν ἀξιοῖς δοῦναι δίκην
ἢν εὑρεθῇς ἐς τήνδε μὴ δίκαιος ὤν.
ΛΙ. πῶς μὴ δίκαιος;

Here μὴ δίκαιος are to be taken together, as the answer shows, but the example well illustrates the force of the foregoing rule.

The following passages μή seems to depend on the condition, although

depende[illegible] all the cases is not really clear. Eurip. Androm. 845.

ἀλλ' εἴ σ' ἀφείην μὴ φρονοῦσαν, ὡς θάνοις;

[illegible] 874.

[illegible] νιν ἔδοσαν, εἴτε μὴ κτανὼν

θέλοιμ' ἀγαγεῖν πάλιν ἐς Ἀργείων χθόνα

Xen. Hell. [illegible] συμβουλεύω δ' ὑμῖν, ἐν

οἷς οὐκ ἔστι ἐξαπατηθῆναι ὑμᾶς καὶ τοὺς

ἀδικοῦντας εἰδότες κολάσεσθε ἢ ἂν κοινῇ

[illegible] δίκῃ, — εἰ μὴ πλέον ἀλλὰ κἂν μίαν

ἡμέραν δόντες αὐτοῖς ἀπολογήσασθαι

μὴ ἄλλοις πιστεύοντες ἢ ὑμῖν αὐτοῖς.

In Hdt. VII 10. ζ. the participle seems to be used instead of the finite verb

ἐν τε τῷ ἐπισχεῖν ἔνεστι ἀγαθά, εἰ μὴ

παραυτίκα δοκέοντα εἶναι, ἀλλ' ἀνὰ χρόνον

ἐξεύροι τις ἄν. cf. Stein [illegible]

In pseudo Lysias XX 20 the position of the negative deserves notice [illegible]

ἐπειδὰν [illegible] κτλ. [illegible] ὅρος [illegible] be taken with λέγειν or with τὰ ἄριστα [illegible] τὰ μὴ ἄριστα. See §§ 5 and 12 where the same construction occurs and where μή undoubtedly depends on the principal verb. But on the other hand in Dem (XXVI. 21) ὡς πράττοντα καὶ λέγοντα μὴ τὰ ἄριστα τῷ δήμῳ. πάλιν ἐκολάσατε there seems to be no other explanation than [illegible] — This phrase is a legal formula and occurs in the speech of Hyperides, Pro Euxenippo several time[s] and in every instance μή depends on the general [illegible]

cf. Col XVIII. ὁ δὲ ῥήτωρ ὢν (αἰτίαν ἔχειν) λέγειν μὴ τὰ ἄριστα τῷ δήμῳ. Col. XX. περὶ τοῦ λέγειν μὴ τὰ ἄριστα τῷ δήμῳ. Col. XXXIX. εἰσαγγελίαν ἔγραψα ῥήτορα ὄντα λέγειν μὴ τὰ ἄριστα τῷ δήμῳ. but in Col. XL [illegible]

[illegible] of these examples, therefore, it seems better [illegible] the passage from Lysias to take [illegible] with ὁ [illegible] as conditional, rather than with ὁ ἄπορος as generic.

The complete list of the passages in which μή with the participle forms part of a conditional proposition occurs is as follows:

Homer
Od. I 289
Sophocles
Ajax 1317
O. C. 976
Trach 411
Euripides
Androm 841
Ion 1301
Medea 242
Orestes 1174
1198
[illegible]o. 874
Frag. 313
Aristophanes
Clouds 415
Wasps

Lys. 1112
Plutus 910
Comici Minores
Eupolis 357.4
Anaxandrides
52.7
[Men 321.15
Euphro 10 14]
Herodotus
II. 13
III. 69
IV. 157
VII. 105
50
139
VIII. 94
IX. 51
Thucydides
III 14.1

III. 46.2
IV. 18.5
73.3
85.2
VI. 23.1
38.4
80.2
VII. 70.8
78.1
Xenophon
Anab. IV 1.14
VII 6.27
Cyr. I 6.22
V. 4.48
5.13
VII. 1.41
VIII. 1.32
Hell I 7.19
Mem. I 2 [illegible]

I. 7.3
II. 1.4
38
III. 1.2
4
V. 23
IV. 1.5
(five times)
2.17
3.12
6.13
Oec. II. 15 (bis)
III. 2
11
De Vec V. 9
13
Antiphon
I. 10
II. δ. 7
[illegible]

III. 5.4
IV. 5.3
V. 37
V
Andocides
II. 1
4
Lysias
I. 38
III. 26
IX. 10
XIII. 75
XIV. 13
22
XIX. 37
XX. 20
XXV. 4
XXVII. 8
XX. 1

Isocrates
(I, 17
24)
III. 11
IV 14
V. 24
29
45
81
105
VIII. 17
XI. 7
50
XII. 23
24
269
XIV. 61
XV. 42
90
129
XVI 48
50
XVII. 1
XVIII. 65
XIX. 32
Epis. I 9
II. 1
VII. 2
IX 7

Isaeus
III. 63
64
VI. 52
VII 19
VIII. 11
7

IX. 27
X. 23
XI. 19 (bis)
38

Demosthenes
II. 23 (bis)
IV 38
(VII. 45)
VIII. 18
IX. 14
(XI. 19)
XVII. 65. 220
XVIII. 201
XIX. 8. 214,
233. 239,
267
XX. 24. 43
46. 113
137. 139
XXI. 57. 100
128. 134
186. 206
XXII 18. 36,
62.
XXIII 42. 57
68. 77
96. 192
218.
XXIV. 35. 47
95
XXV. 38. 99
XXVII. 69
XXX. 23
XXXI. 5

XXXVI. 2. 32
XXXVIII. 2
(XL. 61)
(XLVII. 1)
(XLVIII. 2)
(L. 67)
LII. 2
LIV. 43
LV 33
LVII. 3
44
(LVIII. 52)
Proem. VI. 1
XXI 1
X[illegible]

Aeschines
I. 84 (bis)
131
II. J. 88. 163

Hyperides
Pro Eux.
Col. XXXIII - 521

Deinarchus
I. 112

Plato
Euthyphro 15 B
Apol. 41 E
Phaedo 62 C
80 E
Crat. 439 E
Theaet. 152 D
162 a
165 a
81 B
Politicus 296 B
D
300 a
Par. 136 C
164 D
165 E
Philebus 56 E
Symp. 178 D
Phaedrus 259 a
269 B
(Alcib. II 142 D)
Hipp 226 E
231 B)
Char 175 E
Laches 200 E
Euthyd. 287 a
Gorgias 460 a
461 B
466 E
482 C
486 B
488 a
514 D
516 a
522 D
Meno 71 D
85 E
97 B
(bis)
Hip. Maior 292 D
" Min. 372 a
Ion 542 a
Menex. 247 a
Clitophon 408 E
Rep. II 368 D
370 E
III 393 D
IV. 429 E
V 461 B
478 D
VI 492 a
493 B
499 E
IX. 579 C
Laws I. 638 C
II. 653 B
658 a
660 C
663 D
IV, 701 E
VI 772 a
C
VIII. 841 E
844 C
E
845 a. c
IX. 862 a
872 C
874 C
XI 921 a
923 D
924 B
936 D
XII 943

We see then from this list that the frequency with which this construction is used depends largely on the nature of the discourse. The dramatists and the historians [illegible]

rarely while it abounds in the orators and Plato. But it is just these latter writers, who, from the nature of their writings, have many more opportunities for using the hypothetical proposition, and consequently the participle is more frequently [illegible]. In the same author likewise differences are noted. For instance the Protagoras of Plato does not furnish any examples, while the Gorgias has nine.

Here too, as in the construction previously treated, οὐ is occasionally found, but the instances are very rare in comparison with those in which μή is [illegible]. The retention of οὐ can usually be explained by adhaerescence or by the negative of fact being retained, or by the essentially causal [illegible]

cf ... sentence. Example of adhaerence ex an. Eurip. Iph. Au. 995

εἰ δ' οὐ παρούσης ἀθλία τεύξομαι ἐμέν.

Dem. XXIV. 48. XXIX 36

In Aristoph. Wasps 466. the sentence is really causal

εἰ σύ γε

τῶν νόμων ἡμᾶς ἀπείργεις

οὔτε τιν' ἔχων πρόφασιν

οὔτε λόγον εὐτράπελον

cf also Thuc. I. 124.1, III. 66.2. Isoc. XII. 120. Plato, Sym 185 B. (bracketed ...)

Sometimes οὐ and μή are used in co-ordinate clauses without any apparent difference in feeling. So Dem. ...

πῶς γάρ ... ἐπειδάν, εἰ ὁ μισθώτος εἶναι καὶ μηδὲν γράψαντος, ὅμως δ' οὐδὲ τὰ πολλὰ εἰς τὸ βουλευτήριον εἰσιόντος, μὴ λάβοι ἡ βουλὴ τὸν στέφανον;

ὡς with the participle.

genitive absolute is sometimes found with or although forming part of a conditional sentence. The retention of οὐ may be due to the oratio obliqua force of this sentiment. (see pp. 47 and 5–). Examples are Dem. XVIII 201. εἰ γὰρ ὡς οὐ ... βέλτιστ' ἐμοῦ πολιτευσαμένου, τοῦτο καταψηφιεῖσθε, Lysias XIV 31. Plato Sym.

6. In the Generic Relative Sentence

A relative sentence frequently implies a condition or a general statement. The negative of this clause is μή according to the principle already laid ... p. 16 ... A participle that forms an intimate part of such a clause ... also negatived by μή. It ... to this class that we now turn our ... under ...

of μη with the participle in the generic relative sentence. There are about one hundred and twenty nine participles [illegible] used. The construction does not occur before Theognis. Neither Homer nor Hesiod use it. Nor is it found in Pindar, although both Homer & Pindar have examples of the generic relative [illegible] cf Homer Il II, 30[illegible] Pindar, Pythia I 13 [illegible]

The first example in which a participle appears is Theognis 73[illegible].

ὅσ τις ἀδελφῆς [illegible] ἐὼν μηδὲν [illegible]

Aeschylus has but a single example, Septem, 3,

ὅσ τις φυλάσσει

βλέφαρα μὴ κοιμῶν

Sophocles too is sparing in its use, having but four [illegible]. Euripide however uses it more freely [illegible]

include phrases like ὅ τι or ὃ μὴ χρεών which occur in Bacchae 515, 912, Hec. 282, Electra 223, Frag. 193 ...

Aristophanes has but two examples, Herodotus but two. Thucydides and Xenophon, in his historical writings, use it more freely. It occurs most freely in the philosophical works of Xenophon, the later orators, and Plato.

The following table shows the range and frequency of the construction.

Theognis	Electra 223	Alexis 269.2	VII 74.3	Oec I.16
734	Tro. 1166	Men. 628	92.6	Hiero VII. 9
745	Frag. 193	640	Xenophon	(Rep. Ath. II. 20
Aeschylus	417	Philemon 4.7	Anab IV.2.17	De Vect II. 2
Septem. 3	501	94.4	Cyr. III. 3.31	Cyn II.
Sophocles	784	Damoxenus	IV. 5. 21	Andocides
Ajax 1094	910	2,13	Mem I 2.44	(IV. 37)
O.R. 875	1049		(thrice)	Lysias
O.C. 1186	Tragici Minores	Herodotus	2.41	III 41
Trach. 384	Critias, 4.	III. 132	(thrice)	XXV. 22
Euripides	Aristophanes	" 9	7.5	XX. 1
Bacchae 515	Clouds 619	Thucydides	II 3.7	Isocrates
912	Frogs 358	I. 40.2	Hell II 3.12	
Hec. 982	Comici minores	71 1	33	
	Antiphanes 24,1	II. 4.	1.3.	

Isocrates
VI 61
VIII 22
139
IX 6
XIII 7
XV 143
XVIII 43
XIX 33
Isaeus
III 35
IV 19
XI 29
Demosthenes
IX 65
XIX 161
XX 113
XXI 109
XXII [illegible]

XXVIII 21
XXXI 12
XLV 68
(L [illegible])
LVIII 51
(LIX 103)
Procem I 3
Aeschines
III 226
Plato
Phaedo 61 C
E
82 D
Theaet 155 B
175 E
Soph 219 B

230 B
238 B
C
Polit 311 C
Philebus 14 E
Phaedrus 232 D
(Alcib II 147 C)
(Hipp. 231 A)
Laches 191 A
193 C
Lysis 213 C
Euthyd 277 E
306 A
Gorgias 485 D
Meno 86 B
99 C
D

Hipp. Mai. 290 C
302 C
Rep. III 379 D
VII 533 C
VIII 561 [illegible]
([illegible])
IX 571 E
572 A
X 615 E
Tim. 84 B
Laws III 687 E
V 733 B
735 E
VI 753 C
VIII 829 C
847 C
IX 855 E
873 C

876 B
880 E
881 B
X 885 A
908 B
XI 913 C
924 C
925 [illegible]
926 C

Some few passages of [illegible] of importance deserve brief comment. So Thuc. VII 92.6. ὅσοις μὴ ξυνδοκοῦσιν [illegible]. The only other instance of the use of the participle with μή is Xen. Cyr. IV. 5.21, [illegible] μὴ [illegible] [illegible]. In Thuc II. 3. 2 οὐ is used because a definite body is referred to [illegible] [illegible] ξυνδοκοῦσιν.

Pseudo Andocides IV. 37, has been [illegible] [illegible] the above [illegible] [illegible].

struck the μή inexplicable. The passage reads. οὔκουν τοὺς τοιούτους δίκαιον ἐκβάλλειν, οὓς πολλάκις ἐλέγχοντες εὑρίσκετε μηδὲν ἀδικοῦντας, ἀλλὰ τοὺς μὴ θέλοντας τοὺς μὴ θέλοντας is plainly generic and I can see no objection to explaining οὓς — μηδὲν ἀδικοῦντας in the same way.

Notice further Isaeus XI. 9, οὐκ ἄν ποτε τοῦτ' ἐπέπεισαν οὐδ' ἂν ἐπεχείρησαν, εἰδότες ὅτι ὅτ' ἂν τῇ ἀγχιστείᾳ μὴ ὄντες ἔχωσι τὰ μὴ προσήκοντα, τοῦτ' ἂν ὑπὸ τῶν ἐγγύτατα γένους ῥᾳδίως ἀφῃρέθη. There seems to be no other explanation of μή with ὄντες than to make the sentence generic. It is true the Mss. have ὁπότε instead of ὅτι ὅτ' but this does not alter the construction ὅτε or ὁπότε with the indicat.

a generic sentence is not common. But it is found, as the following examples show. Dem. XX.24. ὅτι δὲ του[illegible] μὴ ποιοῦσιν, ib. XXII.71. ὁπότε μὴ προσγραψάμενος φαίνει, and these are sufficient to warrant the use of μή with the probable [illegible] ×

οὐ is also occasionally found in these generic relative sentences where we should rather expect μή to be used.

× cf [illegible] M.T. §531; Krüger, §67.4.2
Other examples are Plato, Phaedo, 84E. ὅτι γε μὴ ὑμᾶς δύναμαι πείθειν, Rep. I. 354C ὁπότε γὰρ τὸ δίκαιον [illegible] and perhaps Lysias XXVI.10, although there the sentence seems to be more causal than generic, in that it would not take μή. νυνὶ δέ, ὅτι μὴ μόνον ἱππευκὼς μηδὲ κατεβουλευκὼς [illegible].

o Aeschylus Agam. 13.
εὖτ' ἂν δὲ νυκτίπλαγκτον ἔνδροσόν τ' ἔχω
εὐνὴν ὀνείροις οὐκ ἐπισκοπουμένην
(Adhaerescence would suffice to ex)

Also Eurip. Supp 425.

ὅταν πονηρὸς ἀξίωμ' ἀνὴρ ἔχῃ
γλώσσῃ κατασχὼν δῆμον, οὐδὲν ὢν τὸ πρίν
The participial clause is here separated from the principal sentence
Plato. Theaet 195 C. ὅταν ἄνω κάτω τοὺς λόγους ἕλκῃ τις ὑπὸ νωθείας οὐ δυνάμενος πεισθῆναι. Adhaerescence again.
Generally we have ὅσοι, ὅσα μή, but occasionally οὐ is found. So Thuc. I. 7. ὅσοι ὄντες οὐ θαλάσσιοι κάτω ᾤκουν, Plato, Phaedo 104 B, Aristoph Plutus 754.5. ὡς again shows its tendency to take οὐ in spite of the [illegible] of the [illegible] cipal verb in [illegible]

[illegible] participial expressions [illegible]

[illegible] with the participle

were connected with the last two

classes are certain elliptical [illegible]

with [illegible] and [illegible] in

which the participle is occasionally

used [illegible] the principal verb

was doubtless supplied from [illegible]

context and we had an ordinary

conditional or generic relative [illegible]

[illegible] But as time went on [illegible]

[illegible] became less apparent [illegible]

[illegible] because [illegible]

[illegible] with the [illegible]

[illegible]

assertion, with the same use [illegible]

is used not only with the participle

but also with nouns and adj[illegible]

This the explanation usually

adopted for this construction but

for a different one see Madvig Syntax § 206, who takes μή with the

participle as a negative condition

the εἰ being added merely to emphasize

on the condition.

The passages in which the participle

is employed are as follows

Aeschylus, Agam. 1139.

[illegible]

[illegible]

[illegible]

[illegible]

[illegible]

[illegible]

[illegible]

[illegible] Clement [illegible]

[illegible] VII. 31, [illegible] Xen. Cyr. [illegible]

[illegible] XXIV. 116 Plato, Crito, 12 B,

which both [illegible] and [illegible] are

[illegible] although the clause with [illegible]

bracketed by Wohlrab.

[illegible] unequal con-

struction in which the verb had to

be supplied [illegible]

[illegible]

With [illegible] the [illegible] is clearly [illegible] and the parti-

[illegible] seems to have [illegible] by a

[illegible] relation. [illegible]

[illegible]

[illegible]

[illegible]

[illegible] ἐκ [illegible] [illegible]

[illegible] ἐὰν μὴ [illegible] [illegible] [illegible] ἐὰν μὴ [illegible] IV. 16. 1

[illegible] the use of 'almost' all but [illegible] is used and the [illegible] that [illegible] retained [illegible] that demands [illegible] 36. 1. [illegible]

[illegible]

[illegible] secondary tak[illegible] [illegible] after verbs of saying and [illegible] and even after these often they [illegible] an assertative force [illegible] below [illegible] participle depending on [illegible] an infinitive [illegible] required [illegible] use of [illegible] with the participle that we now direct our attention [illegible] subordinate clauses which belong [illegible] have been already treated namely the indirect imperative [illegible] after [illegible] verbs [illegible] the direct [illegible] after verbs like [illegible]

[illegible]

[illegible] the [illegible]

[illegible]

[illegible] ... common ... [illegible]

... appears ... well ... [illegible]

... [illegible] ... xx ... xxv

[illegible] ... construction ... [illegible]

... of the infinitive ... [illegible]

certain ... and ... [illegible]

total of two hundred and sixty [illegible]

... with the Participle

... Clause ... [illegible]

... This Clause ... particular ...

... the infinitive after ... [illegible]

... adverbial amplification

of a pronominal idea e.g. [illegible]

[illegible]

[illegible] ... and ... [illegible]

[illegible]

The first ... [illegible]

[illegible]

[illegible] the archetype [illegible]

causal, but takes πρός [illegible] according to the force

of the preposition.

Pindar [illegible] can have possible instance

of this construction although both

are explained otherwise by [illegible]

scholars. The first is Nemea V. 14,

[illegible]

[illegible] Rumpel, [illegible]

according πρός to the force of the prepo-

sition, and this seems to be a possible

explanation. Dissen however [illegible]

Ode of Pindar, takes πρός with [illegible]

and makes it [illegible]

[illegible]

of the negative certainly [illegible]

[illegible]

[illegible]

[illegible] conditional [illegible]
[illegible] participle [illegible] seems to [illegible]
[illegible] that the conditional form [illegible]
[illegible] and that the participle [illegible]
[illegible] describe [illegible] without [illegible]
[illegible] demand [illegible]
[illegible] the [illegible]
It may be well to [illegible]
[illegible] conditional [illegible]
[illegible] continually [illegible]
[illegible] and it [illegible] hard to tell
[illegible] greater [illegible]
[illegible]

[illegible] ποιεῖ [illegible]

[illegible] with [illegible]

[illegible] XII where the [illegible]

[illegible] account I prefer to take the participle as conditional but in all of these cases μή might defend the force of the infinitive. One [illegible] to follow [illegible] own feeling [illegible] and in two prose [illegible] would be likely to make exactly the same signification.

These passages, as well as those [illegible] under show the difficulties we encounter under the head of [illegible] the passages in Euclid [illegible]

[illegible] ἐγγράψαι [illegible]

[illegible] μή [illegible]

[illegible] the [illegible]

[illegible]

[illegible] ... καὶ τὸ ὑπὸ Πελ[illegible] ...

[illegible] ... the best explanation of all these passages seems to lie in the dependence of the participle on the infinitive clause. It seems that in the first case the participle could be explained as conditional [illegible]

× [illegible]

x

[illegible] XXIV. [illegible]

[illegible]

[illegible] earlier [illegible] though at [illegible]

[illegible]

really belongs to the [illegible]

Similar passages are [illegible] xx. [illegible]

[illegible] the [illegible]

[illegible] to be used instead of the [illegible]

[illegible]

[illegible]

[illegible]

[illegible]

[illegible]

[illegible]

[illegible] and [illegible]

[illegible]

[illegible] conditional [illegible]

[illegible] part of the [illegible]

[illegible] subject the infinitive [illegible]

[illegible]

[illegible] substituted the participle [illegible]

[illegible] VI [illegible]

[illegible] explained by [illegible]

[illegible]

[illegible]

[illegible]

[illegible]

[illegible] which the participle [illegible]

[illegible] on the verbal idea [illegible]

[illegible] which equals [illegible]

[illegible]

The full list of passages [illegible]

the participle with [illegible]

[illegible] clause occur [illegible]

[illegible] 29
[illegible]
[illegible] V.
VI [illegible]
[illegible]
[illegible] 1159
[illegible] 30
Sophocles
[illegible] 1117
O.K. 1110
Euripides
[illegible] 814
H.F. 803
215
[illegible] 549
[illegible] 1288
Medea 339
815
[illegible] 1901
[illegible]
Tragici Minores
[illegible] 324
546
Aristophanes
Achar. 351
Knights 905
Clouds 265
Eccl. 758
[illegible] 552
807
Comici Minores
Archippus 43
Antiph. 187.5
Menander [illegible]
[illegible] 232
132, 11
113, [illegible]
Herodotus
V. [illegible]
VI. 7

[illegible]
IX. 41
Thucydides
I. 42. 1
74. 3
86. 3
120. 2
43. 1
61. 8
83. 5
161
39. 5
42. 5
59. 1
IV 118. 2
118. 4
VI. 76. 3
70. 1
[illegible]
VII. 44. 5
VIII 61. 4
Xenophon
Cyr. II 4. 32
VIII. 8. 11
Mem. II. 8. 1
10. 3
III 9. 14
14. 6
IV. 1. 1
Hell. IV. 1 35
V. 2. 35
VI. 1. 12
Oec. VI. 7
XII. 19
Conv. V [illegible]
Hiero II. 5
Rep. Lac. VIII. 2
Cyn IV. 1
VI. 15
Antiphon
II. x 8
IV. x. 1
V [illegible]

V
Andocides
I.
(IV. [illegible])
Lysias
III. 15
IV [illegible]
XII. 69
XIX. 33
51
XXIV. 18
XXXII. 19
Isocrates
III. 16
58
62
VI. 19
(Bis)
105
VIII. 12
IX. 39
X. 15
XII. 123
147
181
XIV. 8
15
(Bis)
XV. 225
265
259
XVI 9
XIX. 48
XXI 15
Epist. II [illegible]
Isaeus
III. 51
VI. 11
IX. 11
XI. 31
[illegible]
2. 6
IV 15
(VII. 6)
VIII. 76
IX. 64
[illegible]
X 3

XIV. 33
XV. 23
XVIII. 58
100
125
159
XIX. 64
114
218
237
XX. 72
90
XXI. 61
67
XXII. 56
57
XXIII. 122
XXIV 65
69
77
XXVII. 55
XXX. 29
XXXI 14
(XXXIV. 52)
XXXVI. 12
(XLVI. 5)
(XLVII. 56)
LVII. 24
(LVIII. 1
22
25
41
47)
Proem 34. 3
56. 1
Epist. II 1
Aeschines
I. 126
III 68
Lycurgus
§ 24
Plato
Apol. 25[illegible]
[illegible]

[illegible] [illegible]a
Crat. 402E
Theaet. 166a
177a
185a
Soph. 229C
Polit. 286C
295[illegible]
Sym. 204C
Phaedrus 242E
Alcib. I. 114E
Laches 201A
Lysis 216E
Gorgias 456E
459C
460C
495a
501D
513D
Rep. I. 334C
341a
II. 360C
383a
III 389C
394D
416D
IV. 443D
V. 474[illegible]
VI. 488B
D
E
VII. 539D
VIII. 548D
552a
554a
Men. 82a
(Minos 321D)
Laws I. 640B
644E
IV 717D
E
V 730a
[illegible]

[illegible]
[illegible]
V 774[illegible]
[illegible]
VII. 793C
802B
806a
816E
VIII. 879B
831[illegible]
838E
847D
IX. [illegible]
877a
X 890a
XI 942a
955E
961a
Epinomis
9[illegible]

[illegible] from.

[illegible]

[illegible] 1,16; or a [illegible] gerund [illegible] procedure and through the image operatio[n] [illegible] the whole [illegible] this [illegible] the negative of the [illegible] participle. Example [illegible] Hdl. I. 184. [illegible] 158 ×

In [illegible] CCC. viii. 21, the negative [illegible] be taken with the principal [illegible] should have [illegible]

× [illegible] CC. [illegible] viii. [illegible]

[illegible]

[illegible] XX. [illegible]

[illegible]

[illegible]

[illegible] XVI 25 the emphasis on the past [illegible] thus causing the retention of [illegible]

[illegible]

XIX. 21 The negative changes from [illegible] the sentence [illegible] principal verb at the end [illegible] indicative [illegible] started with the [illegible] of using the infinitive but changed to the indicative [illegible] he finished the sentence, thus causing the change [illegible] the negative.

[illegible] explanatory [illegible]

[illegible] particular [illegible]

[illegible]

[illegible]

[illegible] lines of the [illegible]

[illegible] upon the piece of a [illegible]

[illegible] is thoroughly well marked [illegible]

[illegible]

[illegible]

[illegible] unknown conditions [illegible]

[illegible] even when the [illegible] not the

case [illegible] unequally [illegible]

with the [illegible] values [illegible]

[illegible] after [illegible]

[illegible] the explanation [illegible]

[illegible] apparent anomaly

[illegible]

[illegible] longer [illegible]

[illegible]

[illegible] will [illegible]

[illegible]

[illegible]

[illegible] Syr. VII [illegible]

[illegible] VII. [illegible] the [illegible]

[illegible] examples, but even then so [illegible]

[illegible]

[illegible]

[illegible]

[illegible]

[illegible] king [illegible]

[illegible] bestrieted [illegible]

[illegible] used, but [illegible]

[illegible]

[illegible] an explanation [illegible]

See Eurip. readings.

[illegible]

[illegible] resembles [illegible]

XII. [illegible] XV. [illegible]

[illegible] XIX. [illegible]

[illegible] XXVII [illegible]

Plato Euthyd. 301 [illegible]

[illegible] the same explanation [illegible]

[illegible]

[illegible]

[illegible]

[illegible]

[illegible]

[illegible] considerable [illegible] [illegible] appeared to take in the nature of indirect discourse [illegible] able [illegible] the construction [illegible] separate and not [illegible] better therefore [illegible] explanation [illegible]

[illegible] Negative Sentences [illegible]

The last class of [illegible] sentences of our [illegible] we have to deal with the particles [illegible] negative [illegible]

M [illegible] the same as negative [illegible] direct [illegible] [illegible] and [illegible] negative [illegible] dubit [illegible]

[illegible]

[illegible] [illegible] [illegible] ... [illegible] ... [illegible]

[illegible] [illegible] ... Wac ... [illegible] ... [illegible] ×

[illegible] direct question takes p[illegible] of the

negative would have been used [illegible]

direct pro[illegible] ... and also [illegible]

[illegible] of [illegible] distinctive question

[illegible] [illegible] [illegible]

[illegible] [illegible] [illegible]

[illegible] most of these clauses [illegible]

[illegible] with the hackneyed [illegible] not

as a substitute [illegible] [illegible]

clause, but as forming a subordinate part of the interrogative [illegible]

[illegible]

([illegible] direct question [illegible]

---

[1] of [illegible] [illegible] [illegible]

[illegible]

[illegible]

[illegible] direct dubitative question [illegible] better represented [illegible]

[illegible]

XIX. 22, XX. 66, [illegible]

[illegible] like that [illegible]

[illegible]

[illegible]

[illegible]

[illegible]

[illegible] direct for [illegible]

[illegible] Example [illegible]

[illegible]

[illegible]

([illegible] 31

[illegible]

[illegible]

([illegible] Stelle [illegible]

[illegible]

[illegible]

[illegible]

[illegible]

[illegible]

[illegible]

[illegible]

a [illegible] already [illegible]

[illegible] may take [illegible]

[illegible] cond [illegible]

[illegible] occasionally, round

[illegible] the [illegible] and is also [illegible]

[illegible] accents [illegible]

[illegible]

[illegible] 261

[illegible]

εὐαγγέλ[illegible]

[illegible]

[illegible]

[illegible]

[illegible]

[illegible]

[illegible]

[illegible]

[illegible]

[illegible] in [illegible] liter [illegible]

these are simply [illegible].

[illegible] 232 B, [illegible]

[illegible]

[illegible]

Other examples are Charm. 171 C, Laches 180 B, 189 A, Laws IX 856 B, XII. 962 [illegible]

The following table [illegible] a brief [illegible] the result of [illegible] preceding pages [illegible] with the particle [illegible] sentence have been: [illegible]

Author	[illegible]	[illegible]	[illegible]	[illegible]	Conditional [illegible]	Generic Relative	Elliptical expressions, etc.	[illegible]	Supplementary	Subsequent [illegible]	[illegible]
Homer	—	1			1						
Hesiod	2	[illegible]									
Lyric poets, not including Pindar	7	2				2	—	1		1	1[illegible]
Pindar	1	1	1					2			1
Aeschylus	5			1		1	1	2		1	1[illegible]
Sophocles	8	1		3	3	4	2	2	4		27
Euripides	22	9	1		7	11	2	9	1		62
Tragici Min.	1					1		2			[illegible]
Aristophanes	2	3	1		4	2	2	6		1	21
Comici Min.	4	1			2	2		3			1[illegible]
Herodotus	5			2	5	2		4			21
Thucydides	16	2		1	10	1	[illegible]	20	4		62
Xenophon	11	2		5	30	19	1	17	2	[illegible]	90
Orators	14	4	1	13	130	31	[illegible]	15	1	5	197
Plato	40	2		5	75	49	1	63	[illegible]	10	
Total	135	30	4	30	270	129	15	216	17	3	[illegible]

[illegible]

[illegible] ive [illegible] ry ar[illegible] ing and [illegible] frequent [illegible] It begins to be common [illegible] dramatists, and reaches its highest development both in respect to frequency of occurrence and variety of construction [illegible] the orators and Plato. In [illegible] ought [illegible] reason [illegible] the participle could not possibly be involved in such a [illegible] similar to the principal one, and hence we must conclude contrary to Kühner's view [illegible] the principal verb does frequently exert a sufficient influence on [illegible] adjacent participle to cause [illegible] [illegible] when [illegible] [illegible] to be regarded [illegible]

[illegible] doubt [illegible]

return now to the consideration of our subject. We have seen in preceding pages what influence the principal verb exerts on a participle that forms an integral part of the thought, we have now to consider what effect the predication of the participle itself implies upon the choice of the negative.

According to the principle already laid down the introduction of ού, when the participle can be resolved into a declarative sentence it takes with it [illegible] but, when on the other hand it represents a conditional proposition it must have μή. This [illegible]

[illegible]

[illegible] participle [illegible] may appear [illegible] a variety of forms: it may be [illegible] protasis of a condition [illegible] devised, which is either expressed or understood; it may take the form of a concessive sentence; it may appear as a generic sentence with or without the article but in all of these cases it is the conditional element that requires [illegible] [illegible]

The two main classes into which these participles fall are: first those in which the conditional force is actually expressed in the form of a condition, the participle representing the protasis, and secondly, those in which the conditional [illegible]

[illegible]

[illegible] cles, but

[illegible] we take them [illegible]

[illegible]

The conditional participle with μή

The Greeks were not very fond of the conditional participle. It was [illegible] too inexact for them. Hence their avoidance of it in laws and decrees. In classical Greek we have noted about six hundred examples of the conditional participle with which the negative μή is employed. But even when thus negatived the conditional form is sometimes hard to distinguish and this difficulty is increased when as we have already seen in connection with [illegible]

[illegible] acue
[illegible] are also [illegible] in
[illegible] of the [illegible]
[illegible] in antithesis [illegible] parallel
[illegible] with the finite verb, [illegible]
[illegible] being frequently employed [illegible]
out the antithesis more clearly.

It is to this class of the conditional participle that we first direct our attention. The number is not large and the construction belongs chiefly to prose. To take an extreme case first notice how two different authors speaking about the same subject and using almost exactly the same words employ, the one the participle, and the other the finite verb.

In Aeschylus, Septem 424 fol. Capa[illegible]

[illegible]

[illegible]

Euripides [illegible] the Suppliants after

take [illegible]

[illegible]

(? from from this single example

we cannot draw any inference as to

the use and avoidance of the particle

by these two authors. Whether they both

drew from the same source and Euripides

intentionally varied the construction

that he might not seem to copy

directly from Aeschylus.

Take again Soph. O.R. 11.[illegible]

[illegible]

[illegible]

In Euripides, Andromache, 382 the contrast

heightened by the use of [illegible]

[illegible]

[illegible] [illegible] [illegible] [illegible]
[illegible] to ad[illegible].

[illegible] the Athenians bid their ambassadors say to the Thebans [illegible] ξυμμαχίαν [illegible], ἢν μὴ ἐς [illegible] [illegible], but [illegible] ambassadors actually say [illegible] ξυμμαχίαν [illegible] Βοιωτοῖς μὴ ἐσιέναι ἐς [illegible], where μή with the [illegible] [illegible] but a repetition of the [illegible] [illegible]. Other examples [illegible] the [illegible] [illegible] are [illegible], [illegible] 2630, [illegible] 1390, [illegible] 1156, Philebus 42C; while examples in which the two clauses are [illegible] are, in addition to those quoted above, Hdt. I. 187. [illegible] Mem. III. 6. 14. Cyr. V. 2. 32, VIII. 1. 12. Antiphon [illegible] [illegible] [illegible] XVI. 30, XXIII. 110, XX [illegible].

[illegible] 96 [illegible] V. [illegible] v
41 36, VII. 26 x, [illegible] XI. 9, 30 b. [illegible]
rag. [illegible]

These examples show better than any other how nearly the Greek had come to regard the participle as a sub[illegible] [illegible] the [illegible]

We turn now to those conditional participles which stand by themselves and do not have their antithetical or parallel clause to render certain the conditional force. We are then left to the general context to decide whether the nature of the participles. Sometimes the decision is by no means easy as the conditional force is frequently not very strong especially when the protasis is not [illegible].

A clear [illegible] of [illegible]

o [illegible] rek [illegible]

[illegible] med [illegible] d [illegible]

With [illegible]

[illegible] ch [illegible] found [illegible]

[illegible] illustration but abound in [illegible]

the [illegible] and [illegible] [illegible]

[illegible] labialis would [illegible]

make more frequent use of the conditional participle than [illegible]

[illegible] this class is too numerous to permit us to cite all the passages in which it occurs. The following table shows the range of the construction.

Cullke.		[illegible]	
[illegible]	1	[illegible]ophane	
Herod[illegible]		Comic Min.	6
[illegible] not including the [illegible]	2	Herodotus	3[illegible]
[illegible]ndar		Thucydides	4[illegible]
[illegible]	11	Xenophon	52
[illegible]	11	Orators	161
Euripides	30	Plato	202
[illegible] Min.	[illegible]	[illegible]	

Epic poetry is thus represented by but a single example of the conditional participle with μή, and even this is not a good case as the negative goes more closely with the following noun. The passage in question is Il. XIII 2-f. Αἴαντε [illegible] Ἀχαιῶν [illegible] [illegible]

This avoidance of μή with the conditional participle in epic [illegible]

[illegible] of it to a lack of obvious necessity to use it [illegible] settling it [illegible]
by the adjectival nature of [illegible]
participle itself, [illegible] reason [illegible]
already [illegible] made and [illegible]
reluctance to combine [illegible] with any
thing else than the verb.

The orators vary much in the use of
the participle. Demosthenes having
only four examples while [illegible]
[illegible], Deinarchus & Hyperides in the
single speech examined [illegible] not.

[illegible] In the dialogues of Plato
[illegible] we see the same variation.
The Parmenides, for instance, has twenty-
seven examples, while the Phaedrus
a slightly longer dialogue, has but
one, and the Gorgias, a much longer
[illegible]

[illegible] [illegible] [illegible] [illegible]

[illegible] [illegible] [illegible] [illegible]

[illegible] will now be mentioned.

We [illegible] find μή with the [illegible] equivalent to a conditional [illegible] provided that not, if only not, but [illegible] with the subj.

Examples are: (Aeschylus [illegible]

[illegible] ἔρως

[illegible] φέρει [illegible] [illegible] [illegible]

χρὴ [illegible] [illegible] [illegible] [illegible] [illegible]

[illegible] [illegible] μὴ [illegible] [illegible]

γε is sometimes added to strengthen the force, as in Euripides, Alcestis 1106,

χρῆ. οὐ γε μὴ μ[illegible] [illegible] [illegible]

Other examples are Euripides Helena 1052, Heraclidae 764, Tragici [illegible] [illegible] Incert. 166, (Menander Mon. 169) [illegible] V. [illegible] 2. Xen. Anab. 2.7.15 [illegible] [illegible]

Conv. 46. 15, X. 586 E. Lae VIII. 24 B. 44 C,
X. 891 B.

In Sophocles, O.R. 297, there is a construction an exact parallel to which has not been noted. It is the oft cited passage.

πάλαι σε μὴ παρὼν θαυμάζειν

μὴ παρὼν = εἰ μὴ πάρεστι and this full expression is not infrequently found. cf Thuc. IV 85. 2 θαυμάζω – εἰ μὴ ... ἡμῖν ἀφῖγμαι

We may, however, include in this same category of μὴ with the participle after verbs of emotion those cases in which the participle is used after αἰσχύνομαι and is equivalent to the protasis of a condition. So Xen. Cyr. III 2. 16, αἰσχυνοίμεθ' ἂν ... μὴ ... ες. cf. Hertlein's note. Other examples are Cyr. VIII 2, 13, Hell VI 1 44. ...

[illegible] [illegible], p. [illegible] [illegible]

9. 3.

In Soph. O.R. 1368 we have another rare use of the participle

κρείσσων γὰρ ἦσθα <u>μηκέτ' ὢν</u> ἢ ζῶν τυφλός.

The peculiarity here lies in the use of the personal instead of the impersonal construction. It really stands for κρεῖσσον [illegible] σε μηκέτ' [illegible]. As the expression stands, however, the participle may be explained as conditional. Only two other examples have been noted in Classical Greek, namely Lysias XXVI [illegible] and Aeschines ×

The equivalence of cause and condition as expressed by the participle

---

× [illegible] examples in [illegible] both classical Greek of Lobeck [illegible] Soph. [illegible]

[illegible]
writers arrived at the use of μή with
a purely causal participle. It may
be well, therefore, to cite some examples of this construction, to show how
easily they could be lead astray.
Take, for instance, Aristoph. Clouds, 792.
ἀπὸ γὰρ ὀλοῦμαι μὴ μαθὼν γλωττοστροφεῖν.
"for want of learning." Humphreys.
Hdt. III. 65, οὗτος μὲν τετελεύτηκε [illegible]
του οἱ μηκέτι ἐόντος [illegible] ὑμῖν δὲ μετὰ [illegible]
γκαιότατον [illegible] since he is no longer
living, but this is but a conditional form. Cf. Plato, Sym. 180 C,
εἰ μὲν γὰρ εἷς ἦν ὁ Ἔρως, καλῶς ἂν εἶχε·
νῦν δέ· οὐ γάρ ἐστιν εἷς· μὴ ὄντος δὲ ἑνὸς
ὀρθότερόν ἐστι κ.τ.λ.
Xen. Mem. I. 6. 12. δίκαιος μὲν οὖν ἂν
εἴης, ὅτι οὐκ ἐξαπατᾷς ἐπὶ πλε[illegible]

[illegible] ἐὰν [illegible] μηδ [illegible]

μαις. Notice that in each example [illegible] the [illegible] parallel with a clause with εἰ. cf. Antiphon II. β. 4 ἔχειν μεν οὖν [illegible] μὴ ὑπολογιζόμενον [illegible]. Lys. XIX. 29. πρότερον μὴ ἐπαρχούσης οὐσίας (here the causal force seems to predominate.). Isoc. XVIII. 12. [illegible] μὲν οὐκ ἠξίου ἄλλως [illegible] μὴ χρόνιος τούτου μηδὲ μέλλοντος ποιήσεσθαι [illegible].

Isaeus III. 72. ἀλλ' οὐδ' ἐγένετ' ἂν [illegible] μὴ γενομένων [illegible] παίδων γνησίων ἐκ ταύτης, ἐγγυτέρω ἡμῶν [illegible].

ib. V. 16. [illegible] τοῖν γιγνομέναιν, καὶ ἑτέρας μηδετέρας [illegible] λογιζομένης εἶναι, κατὰ δόσιν [illegible] προσήκει τοῦ κλήρου ×

× Not a [illegible] explanation of [illegible]

[illegible] (XIII 6 [illegible] XXXV XXXIX 3.

We see the [illegible] passage [illegible] a few other to be mentioned later which μή seems to be used with the purely causal participle, however [illegible] whose sensibilities for the delicate shades of the language had been dulled to some extent and who were always striving for that [illegible].

Spiker [illegible] VI 323, who says that the participle has no conditional force and that "μή follows ὁμολογουμένως grammatically as the regular negative after that verb". But the similarity of this passage with the others cited above leads us to believe that it may be explained [illegible]

[illegible]

od [illegible] pre[illegible] d, [illegible] ma [illegible]

regular [illegible] causal [illegible]

There are a few rather difficult passages in which the conditional force of participle is not very manifest, but which I think, may be classed under this head.

The first is Soph. Philoctetes 1161.

τίς ὧδ' ἐν αὔραις τρέφεται

μηκέτι μηδενὸς κρατύνων ὅσα πέμπει βιόδωρος αἶα,

The participle is generic, says Jebb, with the usual explanation [illegible] a difficulty (Jebb p. 229 paraphrases so. I believe, however, that while the participle is largely temporal there is sufficient conditional force in it to warrant the use of μή.

Hdt VI.130 πᾶσι ὑμῖν, εἰ οἷόν τε εἴη

[illegible] μή [illegible] εἶναι [illegible] ἐν [illegible]
μηδὲ [illegible] οὐς [illegible] ὅς [illegible] ἐπεσκιρτήσαι
[illegible] differently have μή in [illegible] the participle in the apodosis but the participle really contains a separate condition and hence is negatived. [illegible] For a similar example cf. Xen. Cyr. VII. 5. 56.

Thuc. I. 90. 1. Λακεδαιμόνιοι δὲ [illegible] ἥδιον ἂν ὁρῶντες μήτ' ἐκείνους μήτ' ἄλλον μηδένα τεῖχος ἔχοντα. [illegible] Here μή is most likely due to the conditional force of ἔχοντα. Cf. Plato Sym. 216 C [illegible] ἂν [illegible] μή [illegible] ἂν [illegible] [illegible] μή [illegible] be [illegible] by the conditional force [illegible]

With Xen. Hipp. [illegible] μὴ πολέμιοι [illegible]

[illegible] Χ [illegible] (κα[illegible]), [illegible]

late [illegible] [illegible] ἐπειδὰν [illegible]

[illegible] προὔργου [illegible]

[illegible] παραινεῖ μὴ παραλαμβάνειν [illegible] ψυχῆς

λαβόμενα μᾶλλον [illegible] ἡμερώτερον [illegible]

[illegible] καὶ [illegible]. Stallbaum

explains μὴ λαβόμενα as conditional.

But we seem to need an infinitive

rather than a participle, and unless

something has been dropped from the

text, I should assume that the parti-

ciple here takes the place of the [illegible]

[illegible] cf. Rep. III 389 C, Laws VI 773 E,

[illegible] VI 12 (MSS. reading), where [illegible]

a substitution seems to have [illegible]

There still remain to be [illegible]

few passages [illegible] enable [illegible]

to be used contrary to the [illegible]

VII 4.

οἱ οὐδόμενοι ... ἡμῖν ... εἶσι ... προφέρειν. Herodotus, ... think that Herodotus can ... in his use of the negative, ... οὐδόμενοι ist wohl nur ein ... schen ... μὴ οὐδόμενοι". ... better, however, to explain a nega... tive if possible, than to accuse ... making a mistake ... may possibly be an instance of ad... haerescence, which, it is true, is ra... but ... the analogy of οὐκ ἐθέλω might easily induce ... Herodotus' rather frequent use of οὐ in the protasis may have produced ... cf. I. 212. εἰ δὲ ταῦτα οὐ ποιήσεις, VI. 9. εἰ δὲ ταῦτα μὲν οὐ ποιήσουσι, VII. 10, εἰ δὲ αὐτὰ μὲν ἐπιδώσειν οὐκ ...

[illegible]

[illegible] [illegible] [illegible] [illegible] [illegible]

[illegible], [illegible] that [illegible] to be a condition[illegible] participle — συγγνώμην, [illegible] ἐν τῶν ἄλλων [illegible] πρότερον [illegible] του, ἥκιστα [illegible] [illegible] καὶ λόγιος γέγονεν, but the participle really states a fact and hence οὐ, not μή is used. Stallbaum: "nicht wenn" [illegible] of

Phaedo 63 B. εἰ μὲν μὴ ᾤμην ἥξειν [illegible] ἀνθρώπους [illegible] ἠδίκουν ἂν οὐκ ἀγανακτῶν τῷ θανάτῳ. Again the participle seems to have a conditional force, but Socrates wishes to emphasize the fact that he is not disturbed with the idea of death. So Stallbaum "ego qui non indignor aut quod non indignor". In ed. 1901 [illegible]

—

[illegible]

[illegible]

[illegible]

to be [illegible] and [illegible]
may be due to their influence in
spite of the fact that the [illegible]
[illegible] or we might [illegible]
[illegible]

Rep. VII. 518 C. φασὶ δέ που οὐκ ἐνούσης ἐν τῇ ψυχῇ ἐπιστήμης σφεῖς ἐντιθέναι. Here the use of οἱ rather than μή shows the impudence of these so called professors, denying that the soul has any knowledge until it has been [illegible]

[illegible]

[illegible]

[illegible]

[illegible]

k not [illegible]lly [illegible] for k[illegible] with the participle [illegible]

[illegible]

We must distinguish at the outset the concessive from the adversative participle. Theoretically this is very easy to do, for the adversative ~~participle~~ states an opposing fact and hence has the negative οὐ, while the concessive grants an opposing notion and hence [illegible] × Practically, however it is often very hard to distinguish them, especially when μή may be due to the influence of the principal [illegible]. For example take Hom. [illegible]

ἐπεὶ καὶ τὸ ἐκείνου [illegible]

× Gildersleeve [illegible]

[illegible] the participle undoubtedly adversative and μή depends on the infinitive clause to which the participle belongs. Soph. [illegible] 1110.

αἰσχρὸν γὰρ [illegible] μὴ συναλλάξαντά πως, προφάσεις, [illegible] μᾶσσον, [illegible] ἐμβάλλειν [illegible]

Here the participle is adversative and μή as before depends on the infinitive. Ellendt says "καίπερ μή"; but καίπερ is always construed with οὐ in classical Greek.

[illegible] 2.24, ἐὰν μὴ ἑορακὼς [illegible] ἀπαιτοίη. Here the participle might be regarded as concessive, since it is a mere assumed case, but μή might just as well depend on the condition. These and similar instances we have classified under the head to which they belong."

. the sub . .. conjunctive participle. that one ... to be more freely ... . . another class which all the grammar .. . is place under the head of the ... .. participle is illustrated by Euripides ...

γυναικὶ πείθου μηδὲ ... 15

κλύων

and Aristophanes, Acharnians 282,

μὴ γὰρ ἐγχάνοι ποτέ

μηδέ περ γέροντας ὄντας ἐκφυγὼν Ἀχαρνέ-

... , however, strictly speaking, the participle is not negatived and μή really depends on the preceding verb. Other examples are Soph. Ajax 1011ff., Eurip. ..., (parodied by Aristoph. Acharn. 895), Antiphon v. 16. ...

A particle ... frequently used to bring out the adversative or concessive

[illegible] rally [illegible] ἄλλοις [illegible]

[illegible] αιτιᾳ and [illegible] (cf. [illegible]

[illegible] accompanied with [illegible] and [illegible]

the [illegible] circle connected with it, must be adversative. καὶ ταῦτα is also

generally found with οὐ but μή is

sometimes used. cf. Aristoph. [illegible]

ὡς ἡδὺ πρᾶγμα [illegible], ὦνδρες, [illegible] εὐδαιμόνως

καὶ ταῦτα μηδὲν ἐξεργάσηται [illegible]

Soph. [illegible] X. 23. [illegible] μηδὲ [illegible] μητρὸς [illegible]

[illegible], καὶ ταῦτα μηδὲ ἐχόντων [illegible]

[illegible] πρὸ [illegible].

In both of these passages μή might depend

on the [illegible] conditional sentence.

With καί, however, μή is more frequently found and in passages

where the concession [illegible]

[illegible] cf. O.C. 166.

ὅμως δὲ καί [illegible] μὴ [illegible]

[illegible] yet [illegible]

possibly [illegible] [illegible] [illegible] because [illegible] but the text [illegible] [illegible] [illegible] having the reading of some editor but others read [illegible] μὴ [illegible], which entirely changes the construct. (Other examples are Eurip. Electra v 3[illegible] sq. sq. Aristophanes 9, Aldt. ii.5, ii 3[illegible] vii.214, Thuc. vi.16 5, vii.63 3: viii.73 [illegible] [illegible] viii 1. [illegible] Eq. vi 16. Antiphon v. 54, Andoc. i.114. Isoc. XVII.29. XVIII.25, [illegible] VI.54 Dem XXII.18, XXIII.167. XXXVII.18, LI.– (LXI. 28). Ephes. ii, 12. [illegible] Mitchell [illegible] 139E).

In the passages underlined the participle forms part of a clause that demands μή, but in the other cases the cause of μή must lie in the participle itself. It [illegible] [illegible] [illegible]

[illegible] since all the [illegible] [illegible]

[illegible] the, or

[illegible] may be used or [illegible]

cation of the participle [illegible]

[illegible] is occasionally found in the construction owing to the influence of [illegible]. So Homer Iliad

[illegible Greek]

Sappho [illegible]

[illegible Greek]

Theogn. [illegible]

In the following passage [illegible] is used but the participle [illegible]

[illegible]

[illegible Greek]

[illegible Greek]

[illegible Greek]

[illegible Greek]

[illegible Greek]

[illegible] redw'erw̃ς ὅταν [illegible] [illegible] [illegible] Law: T. C. 4 † C. [illegible] οὐκ ἂν χρῴμην [illegible] ἄλλο ἐγκαλεῖν [illegible] [illegible] ; These would also be explained [illegible] conditional or generic

[illegible] The generic article with μή [illegible] the next division of the independent participle with μή in the [illegible] ticiple or that in which the condition is expressed [illegible] would not appear in the form of a [illegible] [illegible] of a general relative sentence. The participle generally has the article, but the article is not absolutely necessary to bring out the generic force, [illegible] [illegible] Kuehner [illegible] [illegible] [illegible] [illegible] [illegible] [illegible]

. . . . . or . . . . . he take up not to
. upon the reader . . . . alsewhere.
. . . are the most numerous of all
and embraces over nine hundred
participles. With the exception of
poetry it is almost universal.
ου is also frequently found with the
articular participle, sometimes side by
side with μή. The distinction between
the two, however, is generally observed,
namely when ου is used a definite
person or set of persons is referred
to, but when μή is employed the reference . . . to an indefinite . . .
The first instance of the construction with
μή . . . . Menander IV. 31. . . .
Furies cf also Thug. . . ode . . .
who thus mark a distinct . . .

× . Gildersleeve, ...

a [illegible] p[illegible] [illegible]

xa[illegible]ple[illegible] a d[illegible] [illegible] from the [illegible]

[illegible]thew [illegible] [illegible]

[illegible] the Anacreontea and

the Pseudo-Phocylidea have not been

included on account of the [illegible]

probably late origin of these works.

The dramatists do not use it frequently

but it abounds in prose, especially

in the orators and Plat[illegible]

The following table shows the range

[illegible] construction

Authors		Authors		Authors	
Homer	–	Sophocles	14	Thucydides	1
Hesiod	--	Euripides	23	Xenophon	117
Theognis	1	Tragic Min	3	Orators	32[illegible]
Pindar	1	Aristophanes	3	Plato	
[illegible]mother	1	Comic Min			
[illegible]		Herodotus		[illegible]	-

...n ...ence of th... con...unction ...
...le poetry, it ...all use... ...
...Aristophanes, and its frequent use in
the philosophical works of Xenophon
the orators, and Plato seem to point
to the fact that it belongs neither to
the very highest sphere of the language
nor to that of everyday life but rather
to that of argument and philosophy
A few passages that present points
of special difficulty and importance
may now be mentioned
In Soph. O.R. 397 ἐγὼ μολὼν
ὁ μηδὲν εἰδὼς Οἰδίπους ἔπαυσά νιν
this example of the participle with μή
has been the subject of much dis
cussion but is now generally
explained as generic with conc...
... M...

[illegible] tio

[illegible]

Madvig's condition [illegible] XIX. 3 [illegible]

[illegible] μὴ κινδυνεύειν ἤκουσα [illegible], where the generic participle has a concessive [illegible]

A great number of examples can be cited in which the generic participle is used with a definite [illegible],

cf. Eur. Hipp. [illegible] ἐγώ — ὁ

Aristoph. Wasps 1048. Xen. Cyr. II 4 Hell VI.1.11. Antiphon II α. 3. V 65, Lys. I. 11. III. 65, IV. 14, Dem. XIX. 224, XXXVI 18. 57, XLV 38. In most of these the antecedent is the personal pronoun.

Again notice Soph. Antig. 471.

X [illegible] γὰρ [illegible] καὶ [illegible]

KP. [illegible] μὴ [illegible] εὖ γὰρ [illegible]

"The μή [illegible] a logical condition [illegible] concession [illegible]

[illegible] col

[illegible] τῆς μηδ' [illegible]

[illegible] but [illegible] wonder [illegible]

[illegible] Kühner § 51 N 3, [illegible] that the [illegible]

[illegible] emotion [illegible]

[illegible] that the frequent use of μηδ' ἐκεῖνο, [illegible] infinitive clauses produces μή [illegible] by analogy. Clkew says "μηδ' ἐκεῖνο" [illegible] ὀργῆς [illegible] Could we not take the whole expression as [illegible] with ὡς taking the place of the article [illegible]

Eurip. Alcestis 322.

ἀλλ' αὐτίκα ἐν τοῖς μηκέτ' οὖσι λέξομαι.

The Most. [illegible] between μηκέτ' and ουκ [illegible]

Since the usual distinction between [illegible] and ὁ οὐκ ὤν is that the former refers to a [illegible] good for nothing and the latter [illegible]

is actually [illegible] [illegible] × [illegible]

* since [illegible] identity [illegible]

perhaps οὐκ [illegible] would be better [illegible]

[illegible], although both [illegible] and

[illegible] read [illegible]

7. τῶν οὐκ ὄντων [illegible] τῶν οὐκ ὄντα

[illegible]

Christoph. Eccl. 115 —

δεινὸν [illegible] ἡ μὴ ἐμπειρία

though not containing a participle

interesting in view of Thucydides' use

of οὐ with abstract nouns, e.g. I. 137.

4, ἡ οὐ διάλυσις, III 95. 2 ἡ οὐ περι-

τείχισις, V 35. 2, ἡ οὐκ ἀπόδοσις [illegible]

ἡ οὐκ ἐξουσία, VII 34. 6, ἡ οὐκ [illegible]

also Plato Laws, ×

× cf Gildersleeve [illegible] 6 [illegible] contra [illegible]

[illegible]

[illegible]
the distinction between [illegible]
is merely an arbitrary [illegible]
used in the nominative case to avoid
[illegible] but οὐ in the oblique case, where
such necessity, [illegible]
[illegible] first ~~that~~ the passage [illegible]
[illegible] used to [illegible], where
[illegible] could have been avoided by
the [illegible] Secondly it is not
likely that Mnesilochus used [illegible]
[illegible] this, nor can we say
with certainty what he would have
used in the nominative [illegible]
[illegible] in all probability, [illegible]
it would have been οὐ too [illegible]
he wished to negative the noun [illegible]
[illegible]
[illegible]

[illegible] ἔχον [illegible]

τοῖς προφάσιος [illegible] [illegible]

τους μὴ [illegible]

Herm. Stein who, as we have already had occasion to notice thinks Herodotus' use of the negatives is not irreproachable, says that οὐ would be better than μή since it refers to a past action and hence cannot denote an indefinite class. But in I. 6[illegible] we have a similar passage and μή is also used there. Herodotus merely conforms to the general tendency of the language in which [illegible] one apt to use μή than οὐ with the articular participle.

Commenting on Antiphon V 65, ἐγὼ [illegible] γὰρ ἡ μὴ [illegible], Maetzner [illegible] that the participle is causal and [illegible]

[illegible] [illegible] of passage [illegible] cannot

Greek [illegible] the use of μή with

this participle here will be taken up

later. [illegible] the present we can simply

say that the tendency just

use μή with the articular participle

would be a sufficient explanation

of μή here even if the generic force

were weaker. All through the passage

the doer is contrasted with the non-

doer in a generic, not in a specific

[illegible]. For the use of the generic par-

ticiple with a definite antecedent

[illegible] page [illegible].

A few passages in which οὐ and μή

are used in consecutive clauses may

now be mentioned. Isoc. XV 269.

ἡγοῦμαι γὰρ τὰς μὲν τοιαύτας τερατολογίας

ὁμοίας εἶναι ταῖς [illegible] [illegible]

ε — [illegible] [illegible] ... ὡς [illegible]

[illegible] ... δωρεὰς καὶ [illegible] ...

[illegible] ... ἰδίους καὶ [illegible] ... [illegible] ...

[illegible] ... φερόντως [illegible] ... In the former case we have simply useless works of magic referred to, while in the latter case we have a contrast between a useful and a useless class of deeds as the partitive genitive shows.×

Again see Aeschines, 2.104, [illegible] ... λαμβάνων παρὰ τῶν οὐ δικαίως [illegible] ... μάλιστα δ' ... [illegible] ... τοὺς μηδὲν ἠδικηκότας. Here too the preceding partitive genitive shows that we have in the latter case a contrast between two classes [illegible] ...

× cf. [illegible]

[illegible] χόντων [illegible]
[illegible] πολε[illegible] [illegible]
[illegible] ρίους συμφορὰς [illegible]
[illegible] (as the same person is referred to throughout it is rather difficult to see a reason for the change [in] the negatives. Kühner, § 515. 3, suggests that in the first case the participle is indefinite, in the latter the defendants are referred to as a company.

Plato Phaedo 99 C τὰ οὐδέποτε [illegible] ἔχοντα, ὅσ' ἂν μηδέποτε [illegible] ἔχοντες. Gorgias, 459 A, τοῖς μὴ εἰδόσιν [illegible] ὁ οὐκ εἰδώς. In these cases it [is] difficult to see any other explanation for the change in the negatives except that in the course of his argument Plato is passing from the generic to the particular [illegible]

An cor'ng

It is well known the place of the article is frequently supplied in popular speech by ἀνήρ, γυνή, etc. [illegible], often [illegible] in phrases like ἀνὴρ ποιητής [illegible], [illegible]. Steadofst an unpublished explanation of Prof. Gildersleeve [illegible] interpret some cases of μή with the [illegible]

For example notice Theognis, 69.

πολυπλόκιος [illegible]

οὕτως ὡς ἄνδρες μηδὲν [illegible] ἐπιστάμενοι.
when ἄνδρες μηδὲν [illegible] ἐπιστάμενοι.
οἱ μηδὲν [illegible] ἐπιστάμενοι

also Soph. O.C. 73

ὡς πρὸς ἀνδρὸς μὴ βλέποντος

Plato Rep. IV 426 D. οἴει οἷόν τ' εἶναι ἀνδρὶ μὴ ἐπισταμένῳ μετρεῖν. In these latter cases, however, while we [illegible]

[illegible] equivalent to [illegible] the participle have a more distinctly conditional force and [illegible] could also be accounted for [illegible] way.

We see then how large a rôle the articular participle plays in the history of [illegible] with the participle. The other division, namely, that in which the article is lacking is much smaller. We may divide this class also into two subordinate categories, first that in which the participle stands in the predicative position and hence [illegible] loses the article, and secondly that in which the participle stands by itself and seems not to differ [illegible] the articular participle.

The [illegible] [illegible] [illegible] [illegible]
recent [illegible] classical Greek. [illegible]
[illegible] , however, [illegible] [illegible]
[illegible] ×

The following passages [illegible]
under the head. [illegible]
[illegible] are included in the list
[illegible] Frag. 958, [illegible]
[illegible] ἐγχωρίῳ [illegible]
Euripides H.F. 311.

ἃ χρὴ γὰρ οὐδεὶς μὴ χρεὼν [illegible]
Frag. [illegible] Incert. 368, Plato (Alcib. II. 139a)
ἔστι γε διὰ μέσου τρίτον πάθος, ὃ ποιεῖ
τὸν ἄνθρωπον μήτε φρόνιμον μήτε ἄφρονα.
In §4 the same words are repeated with the
addition of εἶναι [illegible]
[illegible]

× [illegible]

πεπόμφασι ὑμᾶς μὴ [illegible] ποιῆς [illegible]
ὑμῖν μὴ κωλύσεις

cf Xen Mem. I 6.5 τοῖς μὲν λαμβάνουσιν ἀργύριον ἀναγκαῖόν ἐστιν ἀπεργάζεσθαι ἐμοὶ δὲ μὴ λαμβάνοντι οὐκ ἀνάγκη διαλέγεσθαι. The antithesis warrants in taking μὴ λαμβάνοντι a general although it could also be explained as conditional cf. ib. I 6.6. Hell. VI.1.[illegible] Cyr. I.3.8. [illegible] ἔσται

Cf Thuc. I.118.2, ὅσα [illegible] καὶ πρόσω μὴ ταχεῖς, see Morris' note

Xen. Mem. IV.8.5. [illegible] known how far the Greeks carried the [illegible]

οὐχ ὁρᾷς ὅτι οἱ Ἀθήνησι δικασταὶ πολλοὺς μὲν ἤδη μηδὲν ἀδικοῦντας ἀπέκτειναν [illegible] Goodgate l.c. 6.5[illegible], explains the phrase as being equal to πολλοὺς [illegible] τοὺς μηδὲν ἀδικοῦντας [illegible]

to be satisfactory (i.e. examples [illegible]

[illegible] all respects [illegible] Din. LV. 20 10

τὸ τοῦτον ὕδωρ ἔβλαψε πολλοὺς μὴ

φυλαττομένους cf also Antiphon V. [illegible]

πολλοὶ ἄνθρωποι μὴ καθαροὶ τὰς χεῖρας.

Plato Politicus, 286 [illegible] μὴ [illegible]

[illegible] εἴδη γενῶν [illegible] Laws VII 806 [illegible],

ἔχει πηγὴν τοῦ φρονεῖν μήτε [illegible]

[illegible] ib. XII 951 D. φαύλως οὐδέν

μᾶλλον ἐν εὐνομουμέναις πόλεσιν [illegible]

[illegible] These examples are not quite

as clear as the others, but the first

examples seem to be [illegible]

passages like Eurip. Herc. 984

ἀλλὰ [illegible] ἐχρῆν

χρῆν τὸν [illegible] μὴ [illegible]

[illegible] ἀρκεῖν,

may also be classed [illegible] but [illegible]

[illegible]

of to bt ... whether ... not de ... pend on the ... actual verb ... they are ... commencing than the ...

... see Crosby ... 994, ... I. 3. 4; II. 1. 15, Isoc. XII. 240, Dem. XIX. 334. In addition to these participles that are used ... the predicative function, we have also a second class ... the participle stands by itself and yet has the negative μή, just like the particular participle. The reason for this ... is often not at hand, indeed we sometimes find the participle with the article used ... with ... without ...

The total number of these participles without the article ... large compared with those ...

but ... sufficient ...
... while ... not absolutely necessary to bring out the generic relation

Examples are: Eurip. Helena. 435,

ἐλπὶς δ' ἔκ γε πλουσίων δόμων λαβεῖν τι ναύταις· ἐκ δὲ μὴ χόντων βίον οὐδ' εἰ θέλοιεν, ὠφελεῖν ἔχοιεν ἄν.

It would be easy to supply δόμων here, in which case the example would be similar to those that precede. ib (Helena, 904.)

ὅσοι προσήκει μὴ γένους κοινωνίαν ἔχοντι κἀγὼ τὸν ... οἰκτίρω γον...

... 209 ...

Xen Cyr. 1.66, οἶδα ... λέγοντα ... ὡς οὐδὲ θέμις εἴη ... παρὰ ... θεῶν ... μὴ μαθόντας ...

... and below ...

[illegible]
τούς, these participles could be regarded as conditional but the subject is
to be supplied from the participle
themselves so that they can very
well be classed as generic.
ib. III 1.19, ὥσπερ ἄν τις τυφλοὺς καὶ κωφοὺς
καὶ <u>μηδ' ὁτιοῦν φρονοῦντας</u> ἐξαπατήσειεν
VIII. 1.2. πῶς ἂν πόλις ὑπὸ μὴ πειθομένων
σωθείη; πῶς δ' ἂν φιλία ὑπὸ μὴ πειθομένων
διαφυλαχθείη; τί δ' ἂν ἄλλο ἀγαθὸν τε-
λεσθείη ὑπὸ μὴ πειθομένων;
Other examples are Mem. I. 1.9. Hell. II.
3.22. Dem. III 35, οὐκ ἔφην ὅπου μηδὲν
ἐγὼ ποιοῦσιν τὰ τῶν ποιούντων [illegible]
δεῖ νέμειν, XVIII 128 (adjective) idem.
Plato. Phaedo, 67B, μὴ καθαρῷ γὰρ καθαροῦ
ἐφάπτεσθαι μὴ οὐ θεμιτὸν
Theaet. 189E. [illegible] μ___ [illegible]

[illegible] ropaer, [illegible] [illegible] sic [illegible] also,
"the use of μή asserts the [illegible] cal tone
of Socrates who avoids categorical
statements." [illegible] of Phaedrus,
264 B, where Socrates is also speaking
ἐμοὶ μὲν γὰρ ἔδοξεν ὥς μηδὲν εἰδότι,
and further Crat. 400 E & 401 D,
where, however, μή might depend on
the principal verb. But there is
also Socrates as the speaker and the
participle could easily be taken
[illegible] generic.

In the Sophistes and the Parmenides
and certain parts of the Republic we
very frequently find μή ὄν, μή ὄντα
&c. In many cases we can see a conditional force sufficient to explain
μή, but in others such [illegible]
seem [illegible] [illegible]ed

to suppose either that μὴ ὂν or ὄν, or else that Plato for the sake of the argument wished to have "the predicate in the same verbal form as the adjectival part of the subject". Cook Wilson On some apparent Anomalies in the use of μή. Trans. Oxford Phil. Soc. 1889-90. pp. 16 ff. For an example of this last use see Plato Sophistes, 258 C, ὥσπερ τὸ μὴ καλὸν ἦν μὴ καλόν, οὕτω δὲ καὶ τὸ μὴ ὂν κατὰ ταὐτὸν ἦν τε καὶ ἔστι μὴ ὄν, also Timaeus 38 B, τὸ μὴ ὂν μὴ ὂν εἶναι, & also such expressions as τὸ ἓν μὴ ὄν in Par. 162 D, 163 a,

Examples of the conditional use have been included under that head. The following are examples of the usage

οὐ γὰρ μήποτε τοῦ [illegible]

ινα μὴ ἐόντ[illegible] ... an a[illegible] ... Parmenides, c ... [illegible] ation of the frag ment of whi[illegible] ... reveals but o[illegible] other similar example namely οὐ[illegible] μὴ ὄντος [illegible]. Other passages from the Parmenides are 238 A, 241 E, 26[illegible] 263 [illegible], from the Republic V. 4[illegible] A, [illegible]

In the Phaedrus alongside of ὁ μὴ ἐρῶν [illegible] we frequently find μὴ ἐρῶντα, used in a generic sense, although in a majority of cases the participle form part of a clause depending on χρὴ or the verbal in -τέον which may possibly have influenced the [illegible] cf 227 C. λέγει γὰρ ὡς χαριστέον μὴ ἐρῶντι μᾶλλον ἢ ἐρῶντι, 235 E χρὴ μὴ ἐρῶντι μᾶλλον ἢ ἐρῶντι χαρίζεσθαι 237 B. C. D. ὅτι [illegible] ... ε

... ipso ...

ment depends on the force of the[ir] participle) 235 E. 2.110, 2.113 ...

It may be worth while to note that none of these examples occur in the Lysias speech, while the articular formulas occur several times. Nor does Lysias in his other speeches use the form without the article, so that we may have here a slight proof of the genuineness of this speech, or at least of Plato's close imitation of [Lysias'] style.

Other examples of the generic participle with μὴ without the article are Rep. I. 332 E, (both with and without

... . IV. 430 B (adjective) X. 599a, Laws III 688 B. VII. 795 B, διαφέρει δὲ παμπόλυ μαθὼν μὴ μαθόντος, καὶ ὁ γεγυμνασμένος ...

o. μή

The following example may also be included here, but in the clause as a whole demand μή figures less conspicuously than the [illegible] order [illegible]

Aristoph. Eccl. 598. ἀλλὰ πέρανε μόνον [illegible]
μήτε [illegible] μήτ᾽
[illegible] πρὶν [illegible].

Xen. Cyr. VIII. [illegible] ἔφη, νόμος [illegible] μηδένα [illegible] μὴ πεινῇ καὶ μὴ πίνουσιν [illegible] μὴ [illegible] Aristoph. VII. 8; Dem. Proem. 56. 1. τὸ δὲ μὴ βουλομένους [illegible] Plato Soph. 237 E, 238 B. C. Cf.

In order to understand its construction we must go back to μὴ οὐ with the finite verb, as the order of development seems to have been μὴ οὐ with the finite verb, μὴ οὐ with the infinitive, and lastly μὴ οὐ with the [illegible]. Under the first head it is used of an apprehended negative chiefly with the subjunctive after verbs of fear-ing and signals. Rather we [illegible] see any grammar or lexicon for examples. From this use comes μὴ οὐ with the infinitive, which is only used after a negative or negative idea, and, at first, only in passionate language. It represents μὴ οὐ with the subjunctive taken up into oratio-obliqua, the negatives being preserved to show the practical interest of the [illegible]

k [illegible] in apposition, [illegible]

[illegible] because [illegible]

[illegible] Because

[illegible] It was always [illegible]

[illegible]ed by Herodotus and Attic writers

[illegible] he [illegible]

ov with the participle is explained

in the same way as the use with

the infinitive. It denotes the [illegible]

[illegible]al, practical interest of the speaker

[illegible] the subject. Like the infinitive,

it is only used when a negative

[illegible] the best authorities

now agree in explaining the participle

in this construction [illegible] *;

although an attempt has been [illegible]

---

my [illegible]

* cf Gildersleeve, A.J.P. VII. 169; Goodwin Moods and [illegible]

[illegible] Appendix to [illegible]

been [illegible] made by Whitelaw, [illegible]
[illegible] Vol. 886 & 3 ff. [illegible] that [illegible]
[illegible] secure [illegible] The examples are all [illegible]
in L. & S. under [illegible]

[illegible]

[illegible] would not be [illegible]

[illegible] which [illegible] all [illegible]

[illegible] troublesome [illegible]

[illegible]

[illegible]

[illegible]
[illegible]

[illegible]
[illegible]
[illegible]
[illegible]
[illegible]
[illegible]
[illegible]
[illegible]
[illegible]
[illegible]
[illegible]
[illegible]
[illegible]
[illegible]

[illegible]

[illegible]

[illegible] readily [illegible]

[illegible]

[illegible]

[illegible]

[illegible] other [illegible]

[illegible] used well

[illegible] turned [illegible]

[illegible]

[illegible]

[illegible]

[illegible]

S [illegible]

The [illegible]

a few [illegible]

[illegible] out of the [illegible]

[illegible] of the [illegible]

of the [illegible]

[illegible]

[illegible]

[illegible] different [illegible] but they [illegible]

[illegible] to the [illegible] and [illegible]

[illegible] accordance of [illegible]

the practice, he only [illegible]

[illegible]

[illegible]

[illegible] and before [illegible]

[illegible]

[illegible] the

[illegible]

[illegible] The [illegible]

[illegible] became [illegible]

[illegible] XXVII.

[illegible]

[illegible]

[illegible]

[illegible]

[illegible]

[illegible]

[illegible]

[illegible] classical Greek [illegible]

[illegible] only found [illegible]

[illegible]

[illegible] the case here [illegible]

however, another [illegible]

[illegible] the [illegible]

[illegible] learned [illegible]

[illegible] the [illegible]

[illegible]

[illegible]

[illegible] of the [illegible]

[illegible]

[illegible]
[illegible]
[illegible] not [illegible]
[illegible] deliver[illegible]
[illegible]
[illegible] the well [illegible]
[illegible] traditional [illegible]
[illegible]
[illegible] delivered that [illegible]
[illegible]
[illegible] doubt [illegible]
by a difficult [illegible]
[illegible] depend on the [illegible]
[illegible] character [illegible]
[illegible] C. N. 14.
[illegible]
[illegible]
[illegible]
[illegible]

[illegible]
would [illegible]
tending [illegible]
[illegible] taking [illegible]
[illegible] and making the
[illegible]
[illegible] influence [illegible]
to the tendency to repeat [illegible]
[illegible] ideas of [illegible]
[illegible] 1130, [illegible] due to the influ[illegible]
[illegible] the [illegible].
[illegible]
[illegible]
[illegible]
[illegible]
[illegible]
[illegible]
[illegible]
[illegible]

[illegible]

[illegible]

[illegible]

[illegible]

[illegible] much discussed here [illegible] with causal force (Ellendt says [illegible]) [illegible] but the [illegible] of [illegible] has been already mentioned. Kühner, § 515 n. 3 takes the participle as causal [illegible] example. [illegible] extended by [illegible] and the indirect question by [illegible]

[illegible]

[illegible]

[illegible]

[illegible]

participle [illegible]

[illegible]

[illegible] absichtl [illegible]

[illegible] nicht well" [illegible]

[illegible]

[illegible]

[illegible]

[illegible] Kenn [illegible]

[illegible]

[illegible]

[illegible] 1886,

[illegible]

[illegible]

[illegible]

[illegible] participle [illegible]

[illegible]

[illegible]

[illegible]

[illegible] remarked [illegible]

[illegible]

[illegible] of [illegible] authority [illegible]

[illegible] explanation [illegible]

[illegible] recognized [illegible]

[illegible] rate [illegible] the [illegible]

[illegible] by [illegible] anomalous [illegible] of

[illegible] cf. X. 2. διατρίβοντες [illegible]

[illegible]

[illegible]

[illegible] participle [illegible]

circumstantial [illegible] would [illegible]

[illegible] § 6 of [illegible]

[illegible]

[illegible]

[illegible]

[illegible]

[illegible]

[illegible]

[illegible]

[illegible]

[illegible]

[illegible] did [illegible] unless we take [illegible]

[illegible] following [illegible] Eth. XII 3.

[illegible]

[illegible]

this example [illegible] the more surprising

as we have had occasion to notice that

the subjunctive [illegible]

οὐ in Greek of the best period except

where the [illegible] demand

μή, and frequently [illegible] the

[illegible]

[illegible]

[illegible]

[illegible]

[illegible]

[illegible]
[illegible] may
be due to its [illegible] [illegible]
[illegible]

[illegible]

[illegible] must be taken with care. Cf. Thuc. VII. 50. 3. [illegible] XXI. 2. 25, XXXVI. 18.

In the following passages [illegible] may seem to be due to the [illegible] character of the sentences.

[illegible]

καὶ [illegible]

[illegible]

[illegible] Χρηστα [illegible]

[illegible]

[illegible] already [illegible] [illegible] conditional participle [illegible] cause and conditi[illegible] [illegible] like [illegible] [illegible] [illegible] We are [illegible] consider [illegible] passages [illegible] classical [illegible] [illegible] an [illegible] participle takes the negative [illegible] scholars [illegible] adversative [illegible]

[illegible] vame ka[illegible] [illegible] la

[illegible] § 511, [illegible] Tayler [illegible]

[illegible] Amoris Regalianum [illegible]

s. xxii. and quite recently took the[illegible]

son, l.c. has made a systematic

attempt to prove that μή with the

causal participle is [illegible]

[illegible] with the causal relation with

[illegible] examine the passages and

see what justification there is [illegible]

[illegible]

that the causal participle takes [illegible]

[illegible] it would [illegible]

conditional [illegible] shown [illegible]

[illegible] because, [illegible]

[illegible] καὶ [illegible]

[illegible]

[illegible]

[illegible] Plato [illegible]

[illegible]

[illegible] with and [illegible]

causal participle [illegible]

[illegible] χωρὶς

ἔχουσιν [illegible] χωρὶς ἔχουσιν and [illegible] to demand οἱ. [illegible] possible, however, to see a [illegible] conditional force in the participle [illegible] might [illegible] might be used because of the [illegible]

[illegible] ἔχοντες [illegible]

× For Matt. [illegible] see page 133 [illegible]

[illegible]

[illegible] could be read [illegible] and

[illegible] a kind of attraction for [illegible]

in which case [illegible]

[illegible] might [illegible]

[illegible] XLIV. [illegible]

[illegible]

[illegible]

[illegible] the participle [illegible]

participle [illegible]

[illegible] γὰρ [illegible] προσ[illegible]

ἐς τὴν [illegible] ἐκκλησίαν [illegible]

ἱερὰ κινδυνεύσειν οὐκ ἔστιν [illegible]

The participle seems to be causal but the passage is doubtless corrupt, cf Cobet [illegible]

[illegible] Lysias 10 [illegible] and [illegible] 9, 13 are also apparently causal [illegible] are not included on account of [illegible] character of these [illegible] place than that the passage in which [illegible]

[illegible] Mem [illegible] 133, Antiphon [illegible]

Antiphon V. 65 [illegible] XXV [illegible] 9[illegible]

[illegible]

[illegible] Nixon's article, [illegible]

[illegible]

[illegible] connection with those in [illegible]

[illegible] could be [illegible] that was the correct [illegible] of the causal principle

[illegible] the result of [illegible]

[illegible] with [illegible]

[illegible]

	[illegible]	[illegible]	[illegible]	[illegible]	[illegible]	[illegible]	[illegible]
		1					
Homerische Hymnen							
Hesiod							
[illegible]		.		2			
Pindar				1			
Aeschylus		11		6			
Sophocles	1	11	2	14			[illegible]
Euripides	1	36	3	23	3	2	
Tragici Min.		4	1	3	1		
Aristophanes		5	3	3	1	1	
Comici Min.	×11	6		1			×1
Herodotus	1	30	3	14			?
Thucydides	1	42	3	49			
Xenophon	3	52	2	114	7	12	
Oratores	1	161	10	322	4	3	1
Plato	13	202	4	367	3	31	1
Total	341	561	31	926	14	56	8

× [illegible] Tillmann, [illegible]

We are then in the latter adjustion, in the case of the dependent having all some that of the dependent construction what little used up and lyric poetry but begin to be enlarged quite freely by the dra-matists after whom [illegible] according [illegible] common. The two main [illegible] of development are the term conditional and the general participle with [illegible]

Conclusion

We can now set up at [illegible] the two tables, Nos. 18 and 19 [illegible] respectively which show us the dependent and independent uses of [illegible] with the participle.

FOLD OUT

it was then [illegible] had [illegible] to

ly, one hundred and twenty [illegible]

[illegible] of [illegible] with the [illegible]

([illegible] about one third [illegible]

[illegible] for the special [illegible]

in [illegible] negative to the principal [illegible]

[illegible] which they depend, [illegible]

remaining two thirds [illegible] the [illegible]

of the participle itself [illegible]

[illegible]. At the bottom of this [illegible]

found to lie the conditional [illegible]

[illegible] although the participle may be

[illegible] under the [illegible]

[illegible] in addition [illegible]

[illegible]

[illegible]

[illegible]

[illegible] of [illegible]

[illegible]

[illegible] of fact. [illegible]
[illegible] [illegible] [illegible]
[illegible] analier cannot be [illegible]
[illegible] [illegible]
Special attention [illegible]
to the pregnancy with [illegible]
condition [illegible]
[illegible] later [illegible]
[illegible] habit [illegible]
[illegible] cannot [illegible]
We regret also to notice [illegible]
[illegible] of the supplementary [illegible]
the [illegible] infrequent [illegible] from [illegible]
[illegible] with [illegible]
after [illegible] of [illegible] and [illegible]
[illegible] will of the [illegible]
this was also another point [illegible]
the [illegible] with [illegible]
made inroads on the [illegible]

[illegible] to the [illegible]usage of the individual [illegible]
shows but little to be [illegible] [illegible]
[illegible] [illegible] [illegible] on account
of the absence of a suitable basis
of comparison, a page of poetry not
being by any means equal to a
page of prose. Still we may gather
from the accompanying table some
points of interest and profit.
Notice first the almost entire absence of the construction [illegible] in
poetry and its small use [illegible] [illegible]
Doubtless the themes treated had
much to do with this infrequent
use but it also seems probable
that in this early literature [illegible]
[illegible] itself was not put to [illegible]
so good a substitute [illegible] [illegible] to
[illegible] [illegible]

[illegible]

[illegible] dramatic poetry, and [illegible]

Sophocles that are [illegible] con-

tion used with any [illegible]

[illegible] dramatic poet [illegible]

[illegible] found in the use of [illegible]

the participle, counting [illegible]

for Aeschylus, 10000 for Sophocles

26000 for Euripides, and [illegible] for

Aristophanes, the average per 10000

[illegible] without counting [illegible]

lines from the fragments, [illegible] Aeschy-

lus 36, Sophocles 61, Euripides [illegible], and

Aristophanes 24. [illegible]

[illegible] small use [illegible] Aristotle [illegible]

participle itself [illegible]

had reached the full [illegible]

[illegible] must be due to [illegible]

[illegible]

[illegible] a X[illegible] [illegible]

[illegible] collection [illegible]

[illegible] Thucydides [illegible] or

[illegible]cydides, while [illegible]

fall [illegible] below [illegible] letters.

Xenophon has an average of [illegible] one hundred twelve pages, Herodotus 41 and Thucydides 26, [illegible] coincides with the [illegible] of the [illegible] of the [illegible] writers, [illegible] accumulative [illegible] of letters. Of the orators Antiphon [illegible] has the highest average, having 62 examples [illegible] hundred pages [illegible] with but [illegible] averages of others are as follows: [illegible]

[illegible]

Unabain

ragir Zu t

While lat

cratory and

Participle

Lapsement.

Su from

ty increase

ticiple,

umber of

to the car

[illegible]

[illegible]

[illegible]

[illegible]

[illegible] und Modus im Griechischen, [illegible]

Bäumlein Untersuchungen über Griechische Partikeln, Stuttgart, [illegible]

Kühner Ausführliche Grammatik [illegible]

Madvig Syntax der Griechischen Sprache. Braunschweig [illegible]

Goodwin Moods and Tenses, Boston 1890

Krüger [illegible]-Griechische Sprachlehre

[illegible]

In addition to the articles [illegible]

[illegible]

[illegible]

[illegible]

[illegible]

Wil[illegible] [illegible] [illegible] [illegible] [illegible] born at Baltimore, Maryland, on the [illegible] day of September 1867. His preliminary education was acquired chiefly in the public schools of Baltimore. In June, 1885, he entered the Johns Hopkins University and pursued the classical group of studies, receiving the degree of Bachelor of Arts in June, 1891. Since then he has been engaged in graduate work in Greek, Latin, and Sanskrit under the direction of Professors Gildersleeve, Warren and Bloomfield, to whom he is deeply [illegible] for the guidance and instruction [illegible] him. During his residence at the University he was [illegible] [illegible] Scholar, 1888-89, Honorary Scholar, 1889-91, University Scholar, 1891-93, Fellow in Greek 1893-94 and Fellow by Courtesy, [illegible]

www.ingramcontent.com/pod-product-compliance
Lightning Source LLC
Chambersburg PA
CBHW050851300426
44111CB00010B/1209

* 9 7 8 3 3 3 7 7 3 1 0 1 4 *